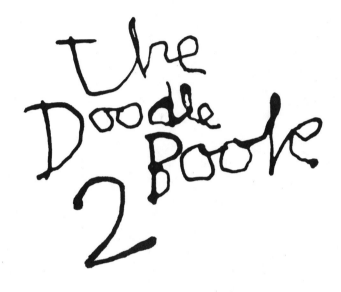

Translated from the Japanese *Rakugaki* 2 by Moko S. Tanaka Kelley

First published in the United Kingdom in 2005
Thames & Hudson Ltd, 181A High Holborn, London WC1V 7QX

www.thamesandhudson.com

© 2005 Thames & Hudson Ltd, London
Original edition © 1992 Taro Gomi

Reprinted 2006

British Library Cataloguing-in-Publication Data
A catalogue record for this book is available from the British Library

ISBN-13: 978-0-500-28567-1
ISBN-10: 0-500-28567-5

Printed and bound in Singapore

The Doodle 2 Book

draw!
colour!
create!

Taro Gomi

Thames & Hudson

Build the wall as high as you can

Ask your friend to help

Don't use a tractor – that's cheating!

Make them yummy

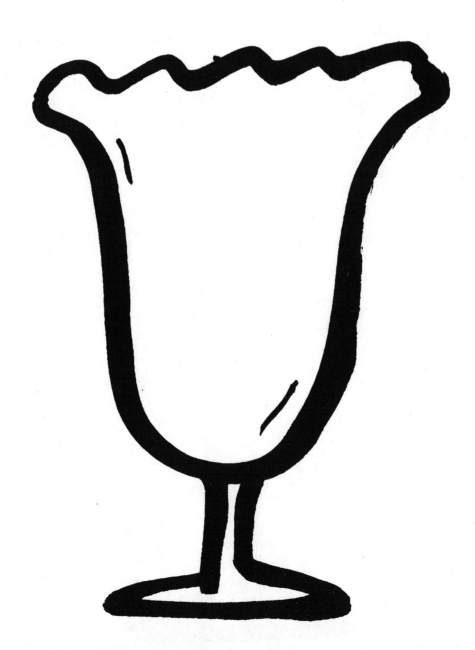

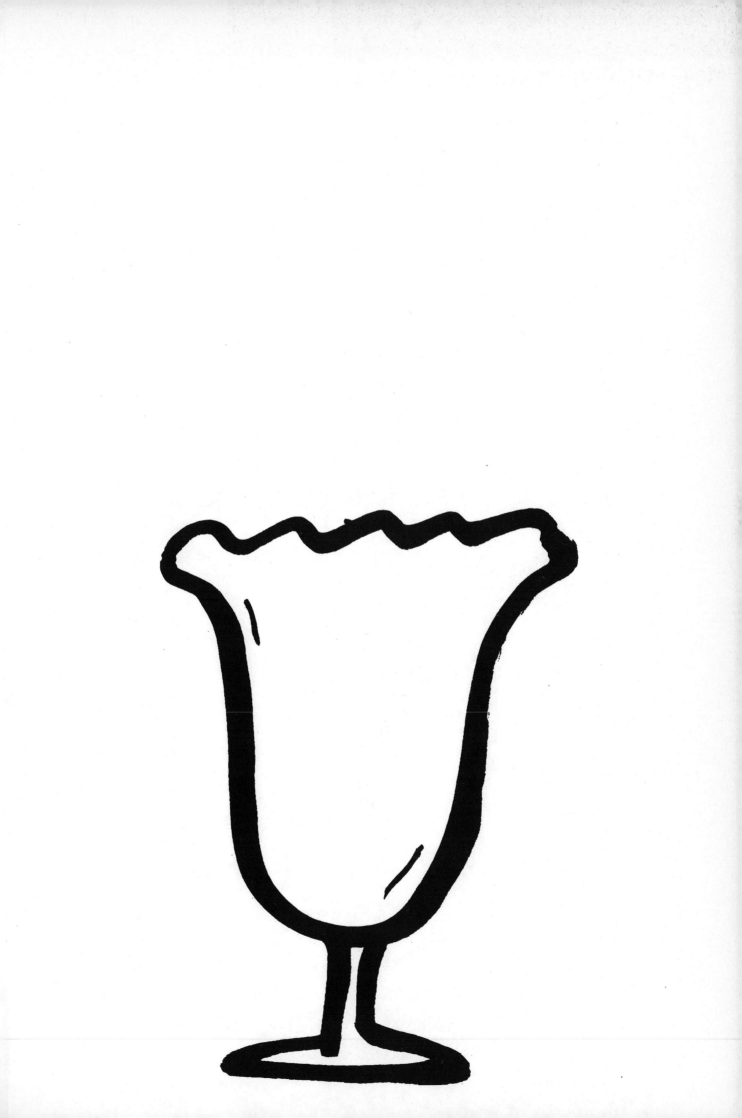

Guess what your friend would like

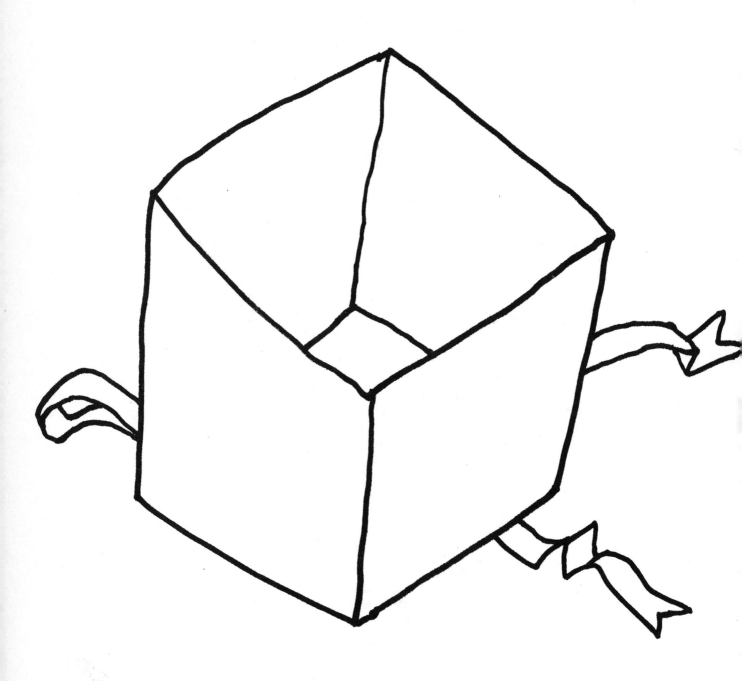

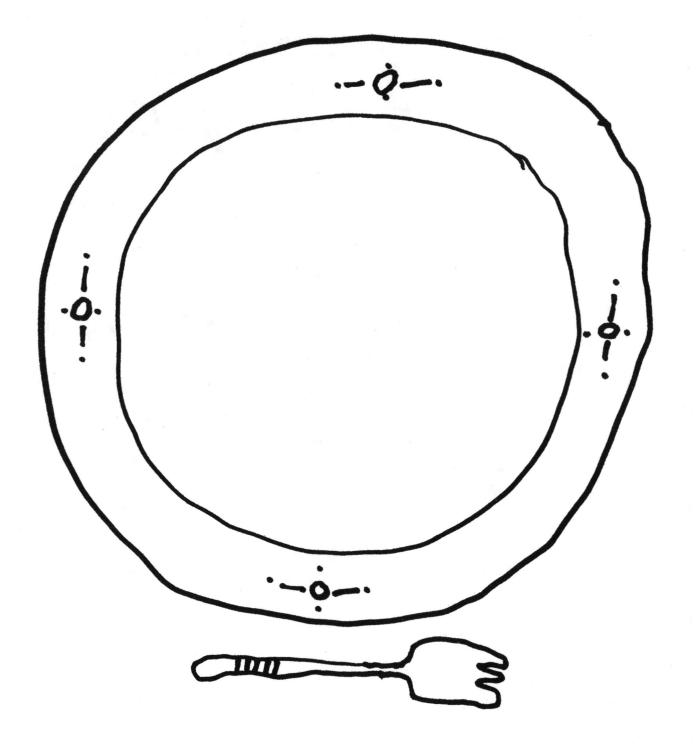

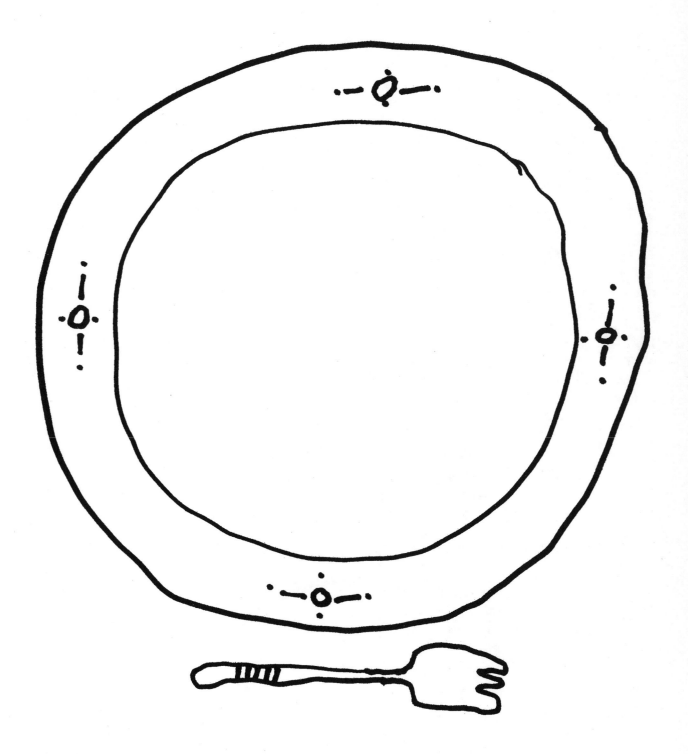

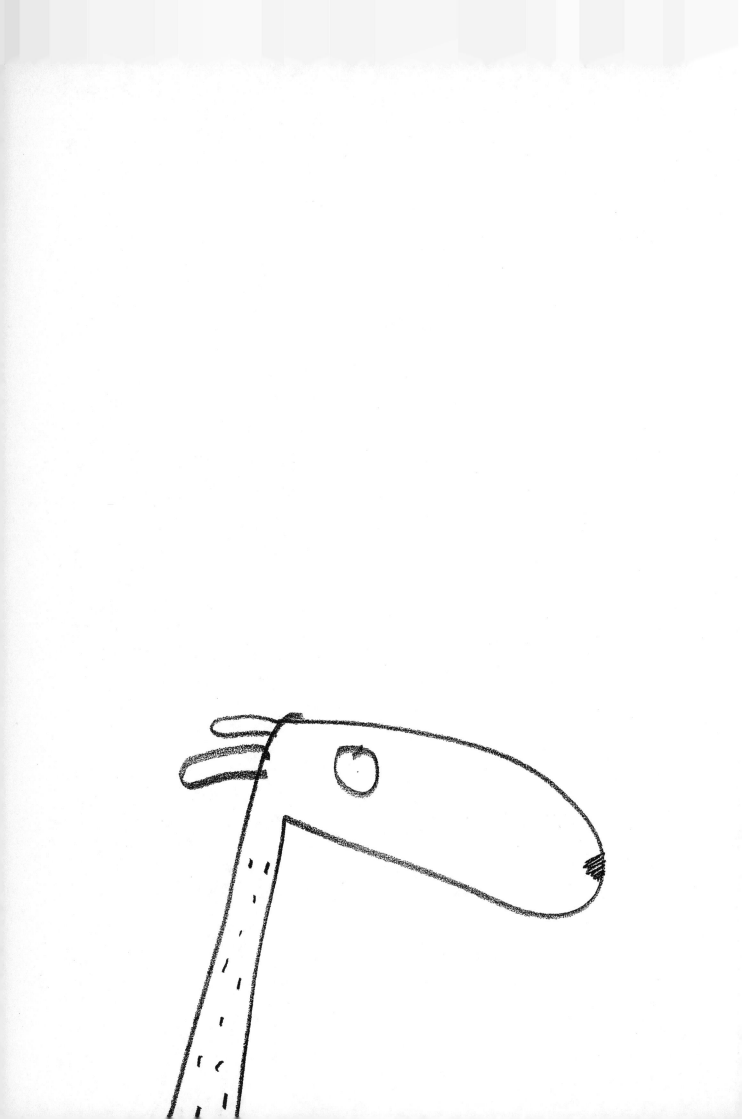

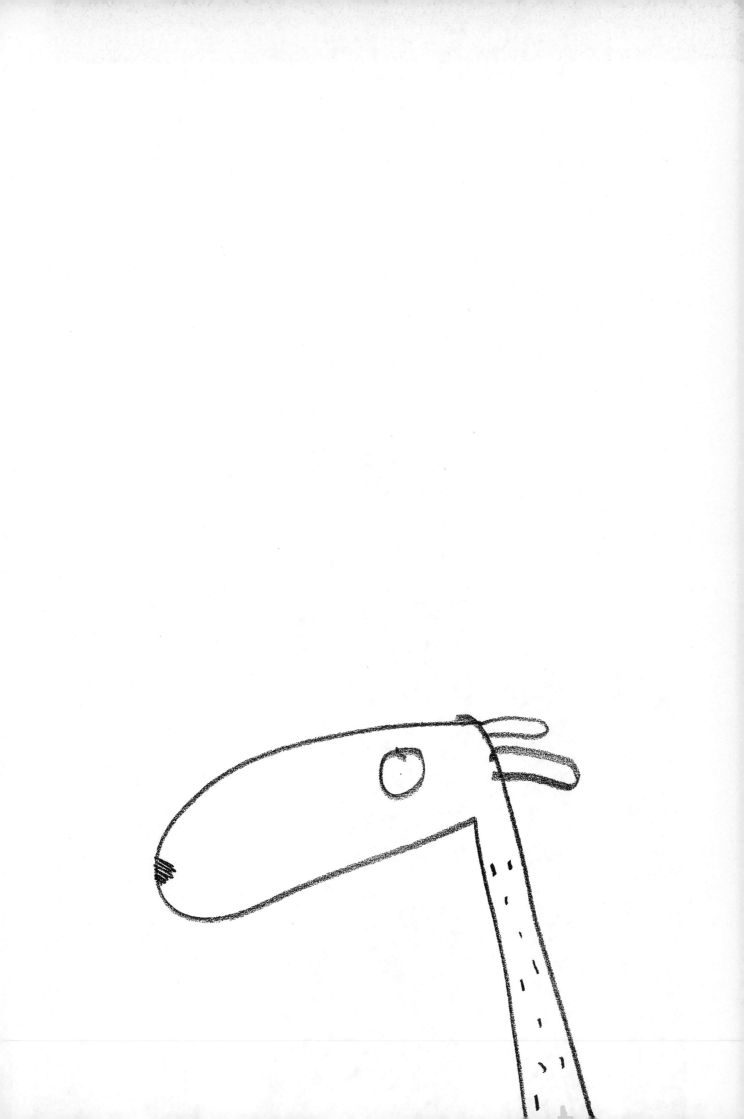

Decorate this restaurant

Make it look nicer than the one next door

Guess what's growing

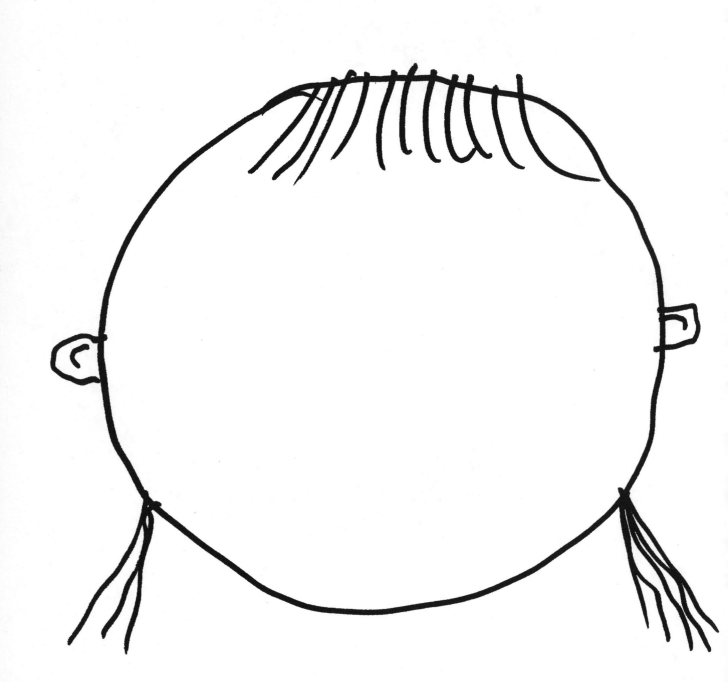

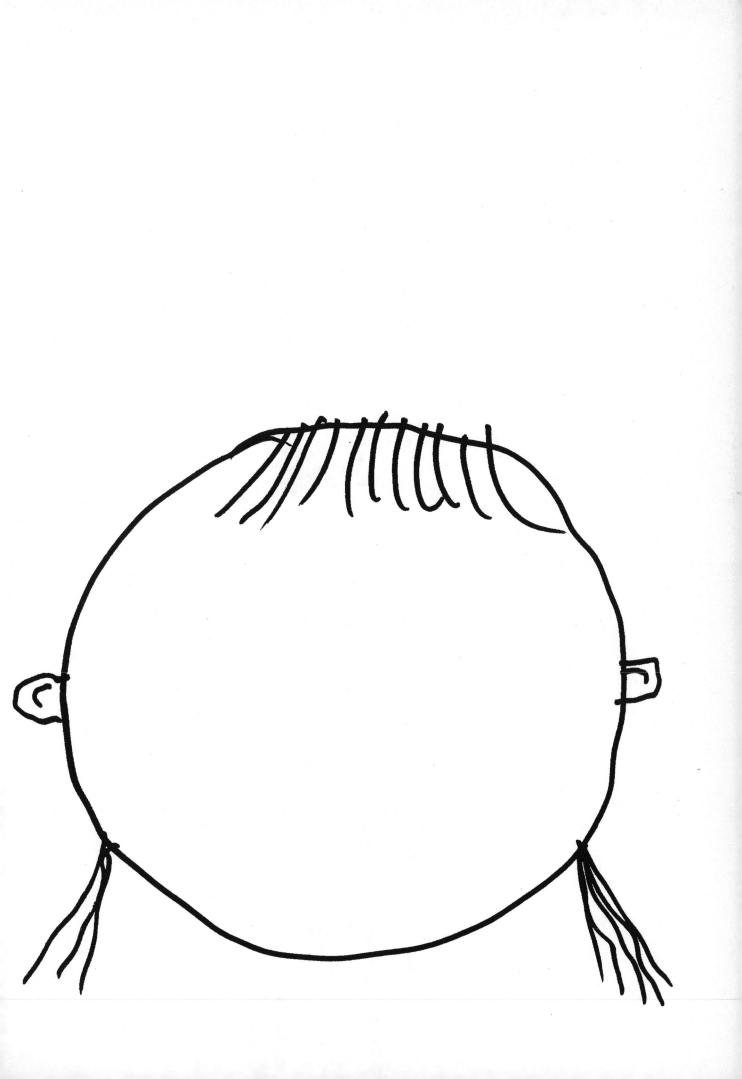

It's raining!

Draw the raindrops

Surprise us with your magic

They are very long...

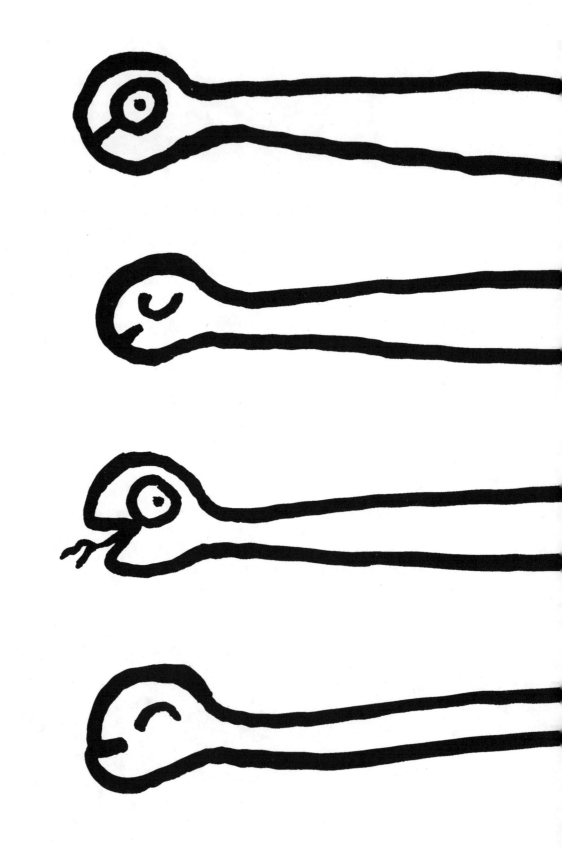

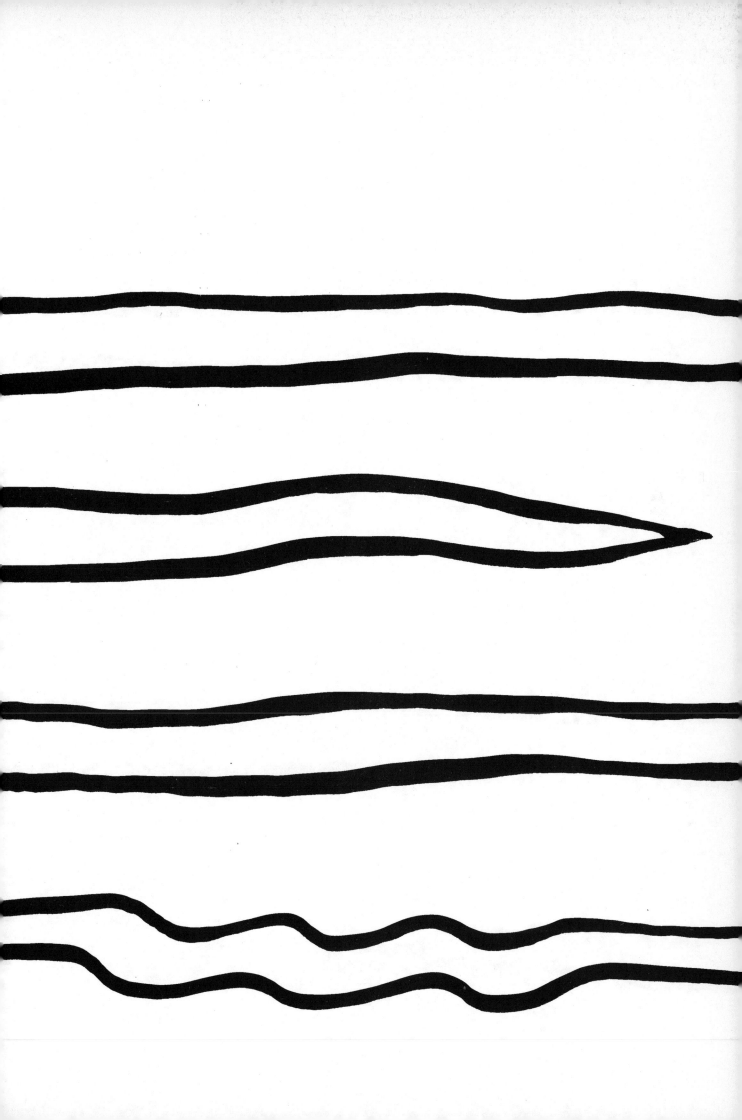

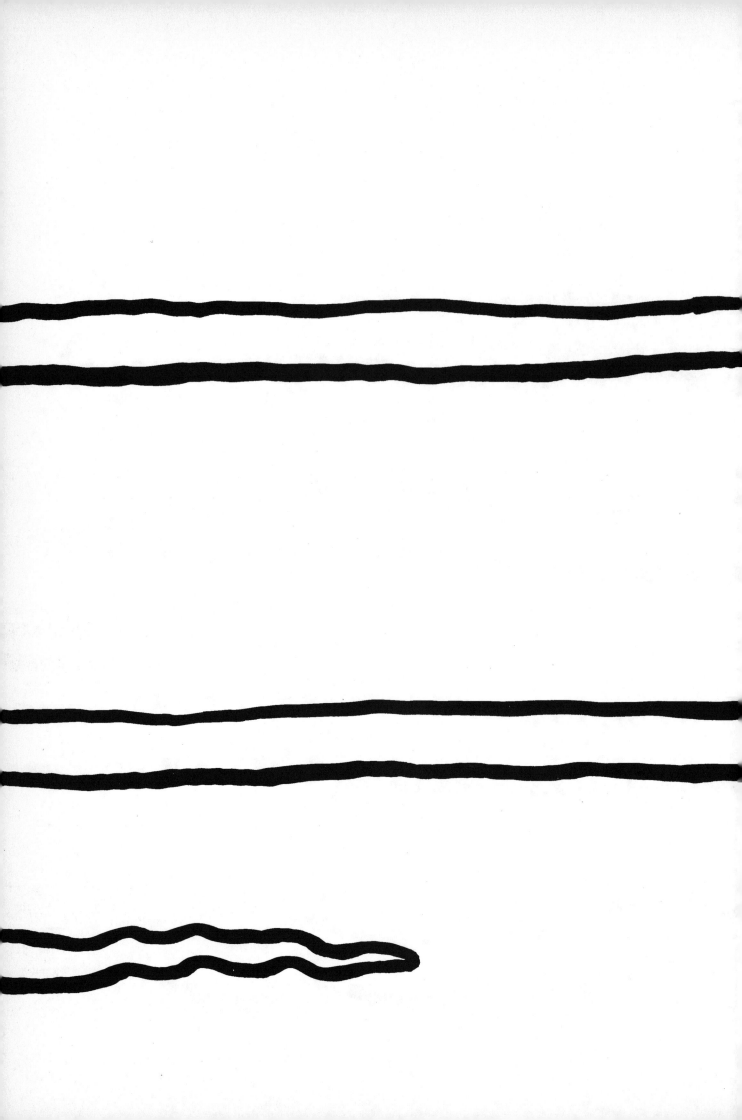

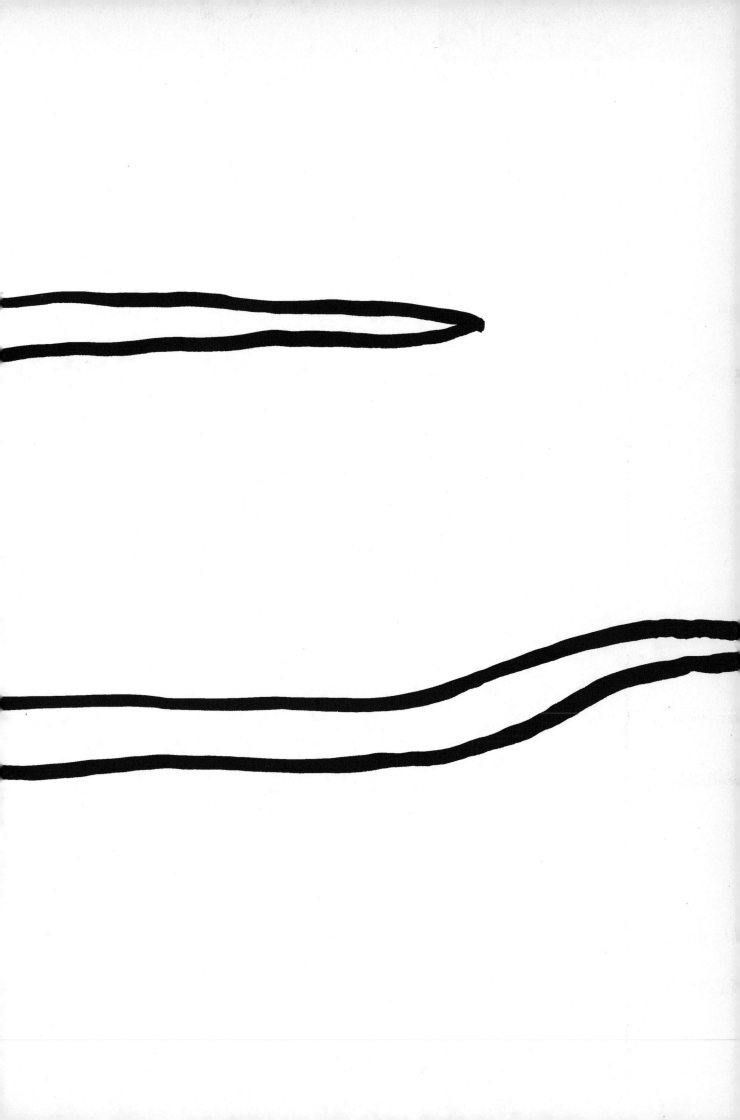

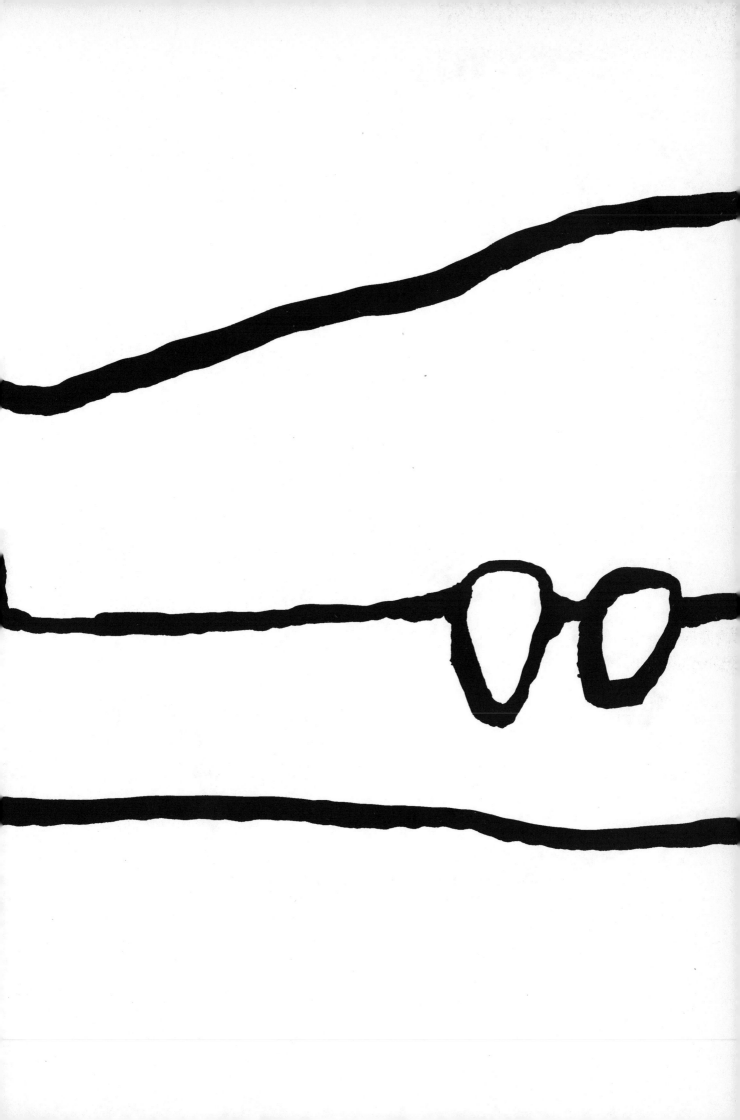

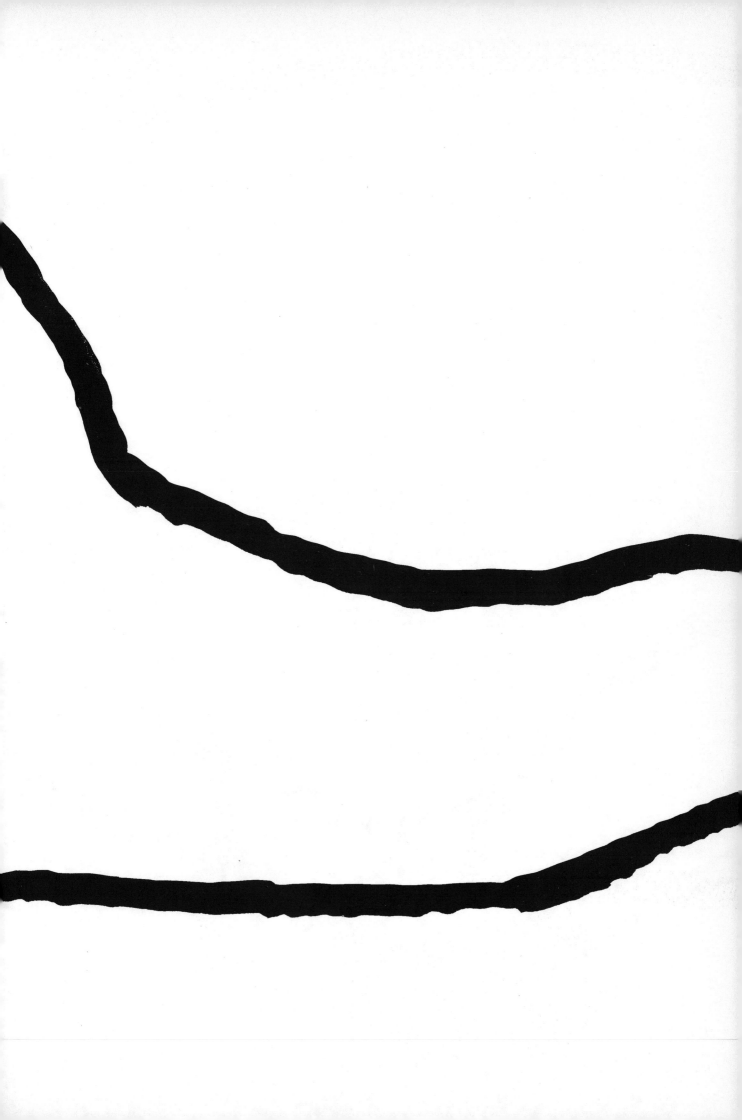

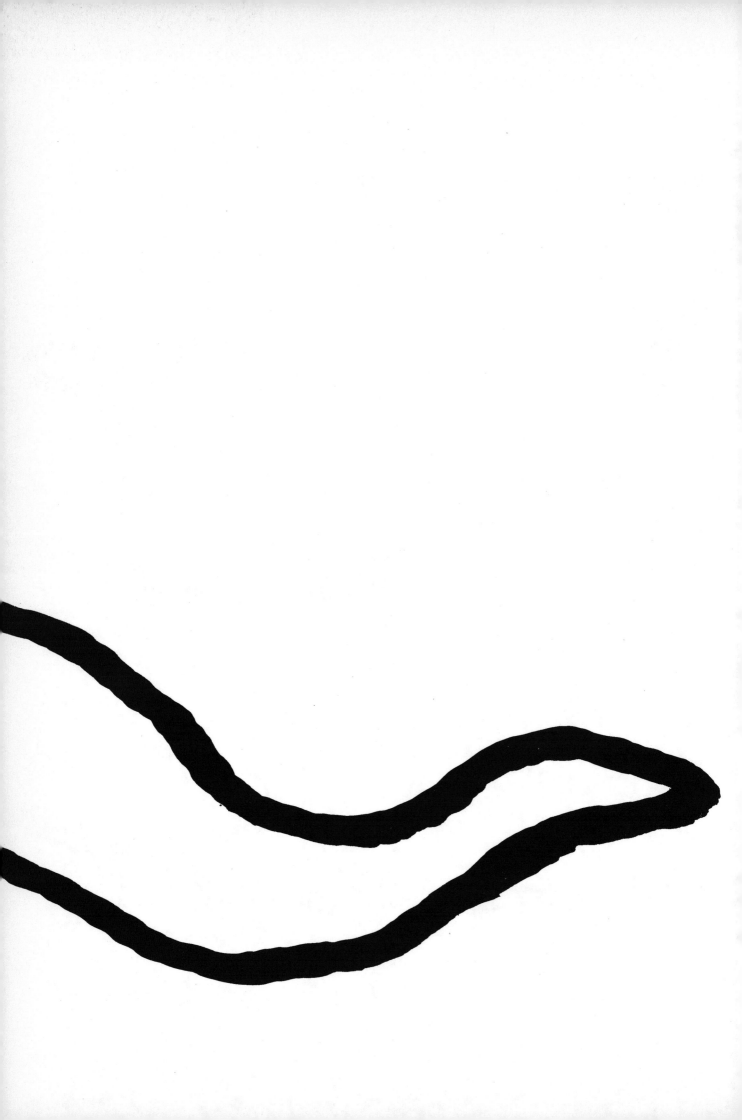

It's a good job it's not life-size. It would take up the entire book!

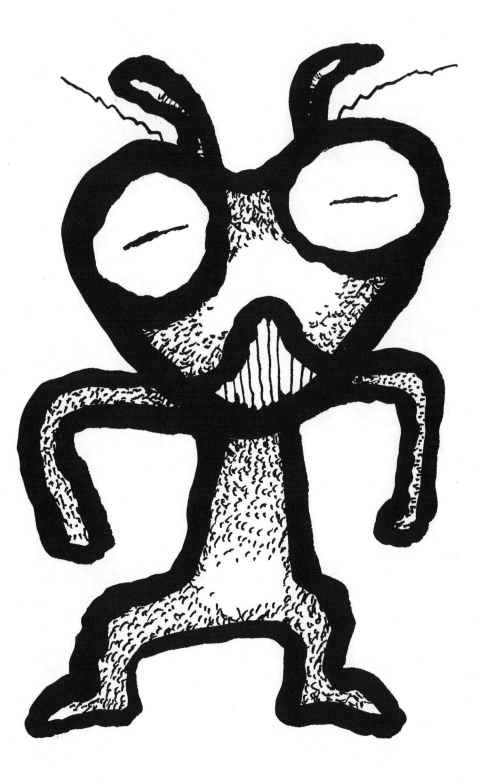

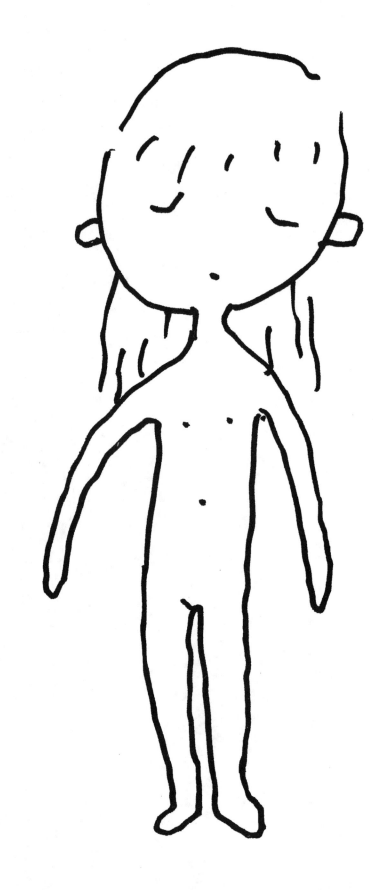

Make them cool!

The elephants are worried

Can you guess why?

A grocer and a fishmonger

Draw a sign and some goods for each shop...
And draw some customers too

Draw the number 85

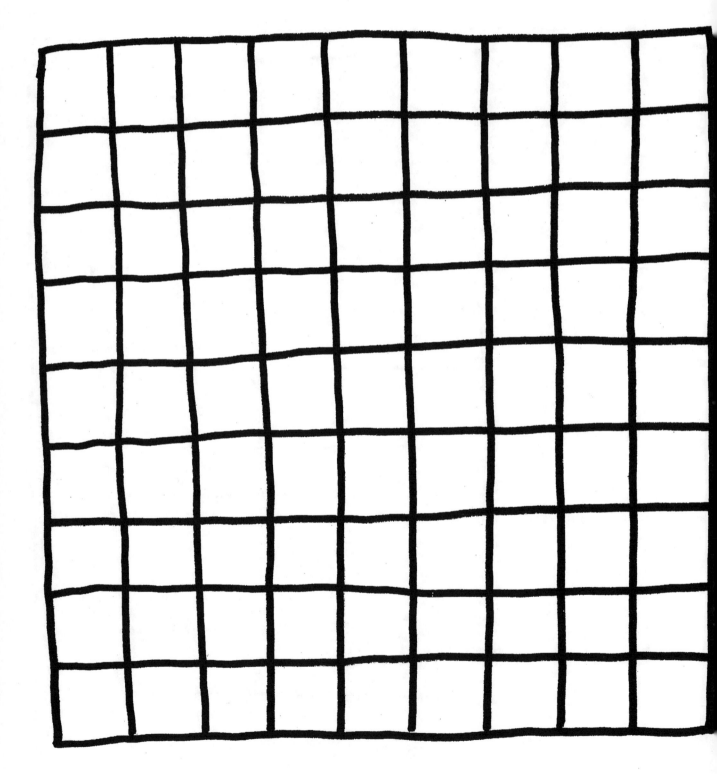

Draw the first letter of your name

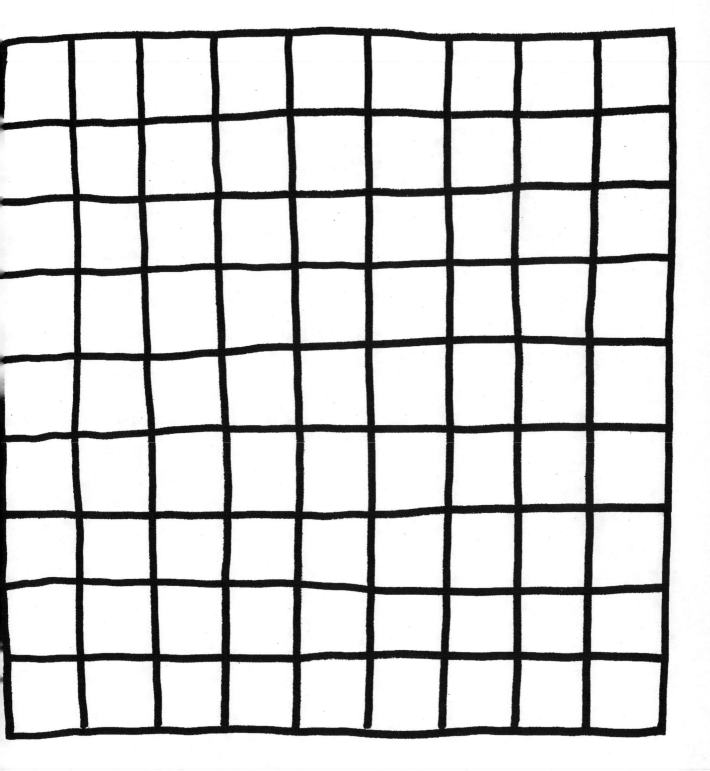

Give them shoes

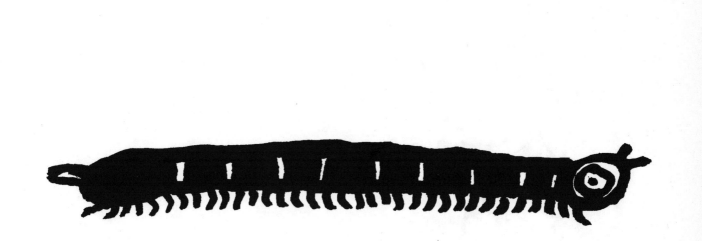

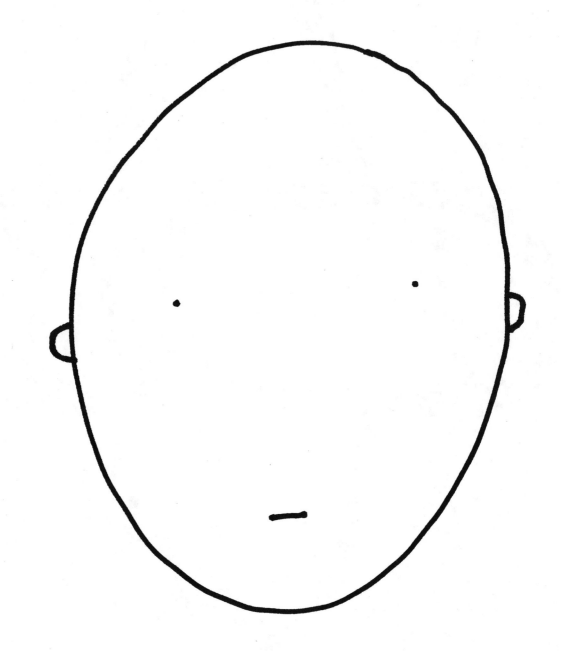

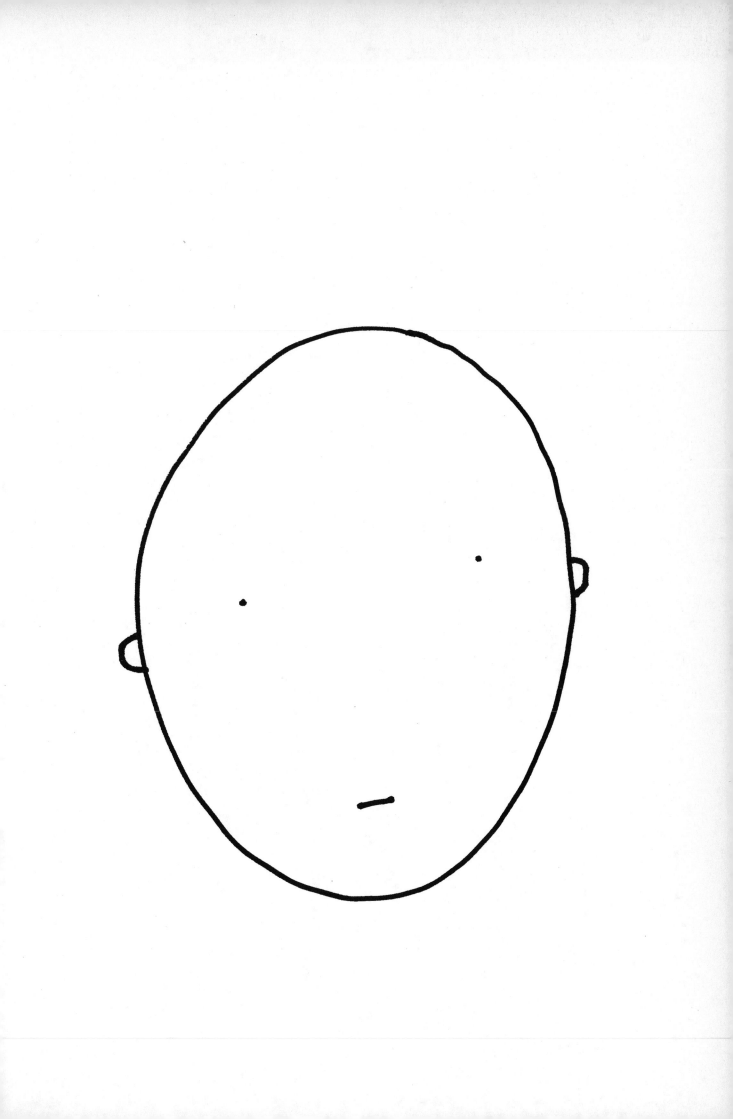

Then draw it on the uniform

Make up a story and write it down
Think of a good title too

Written by ....
Illustrated by Taro Gomi

Published by
The Doodle Book

The end

ISBN4-89234-002-4

C0011 P60E

The Doodle Book

← This is the back cover
of your picture book.
Cut out the pages to
make the book!

If you think it's any good,
send it to:
The Doodle Book
1 Iceberg Street
North Pole

Draw some flowers, leaves and people

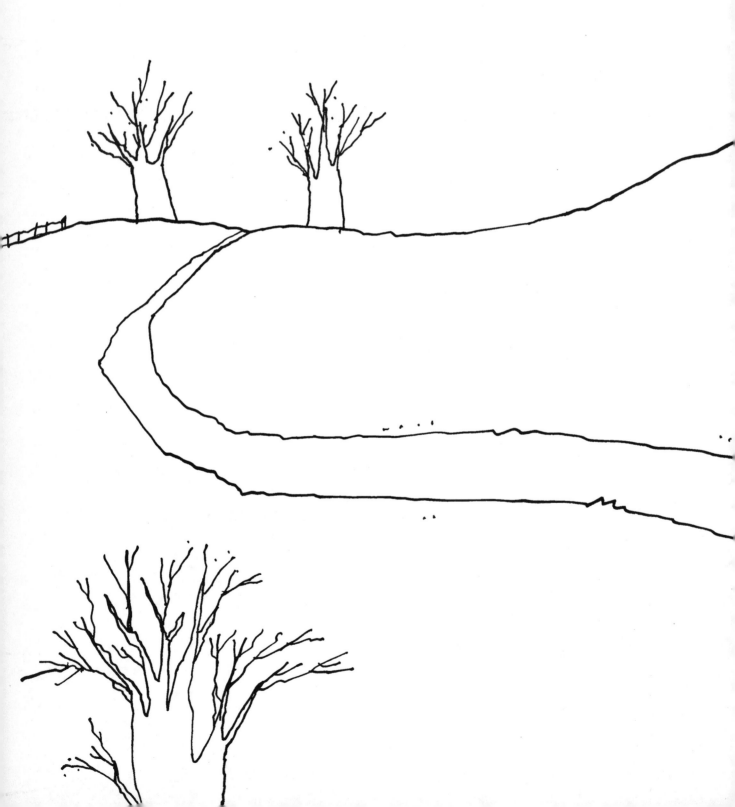

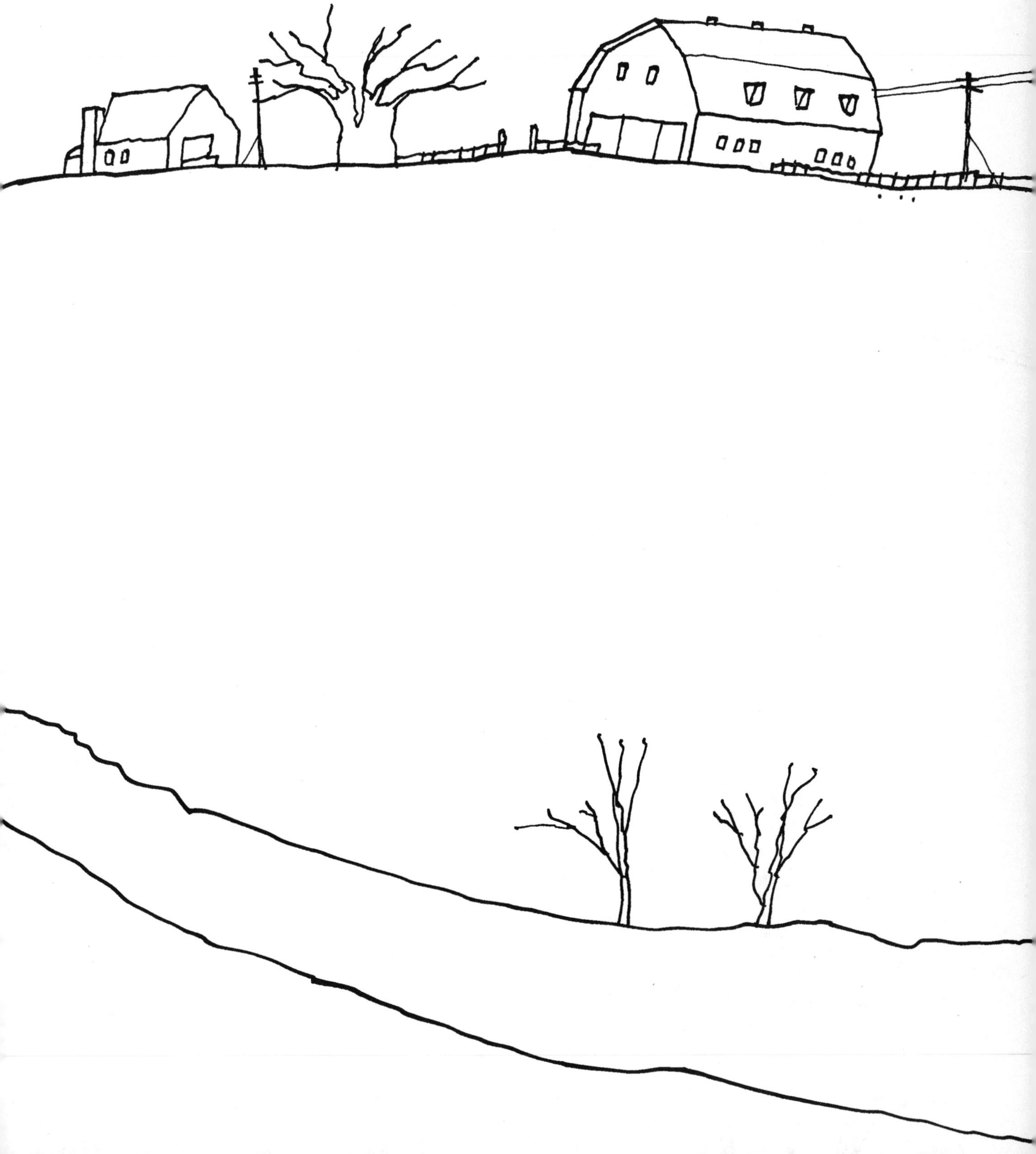

It's summer now

Make it summery

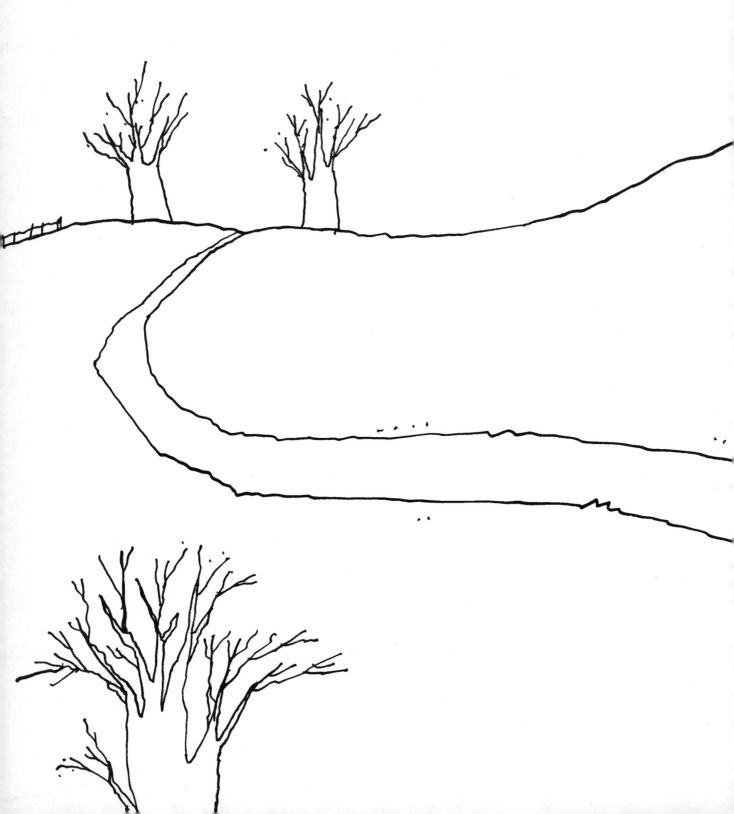

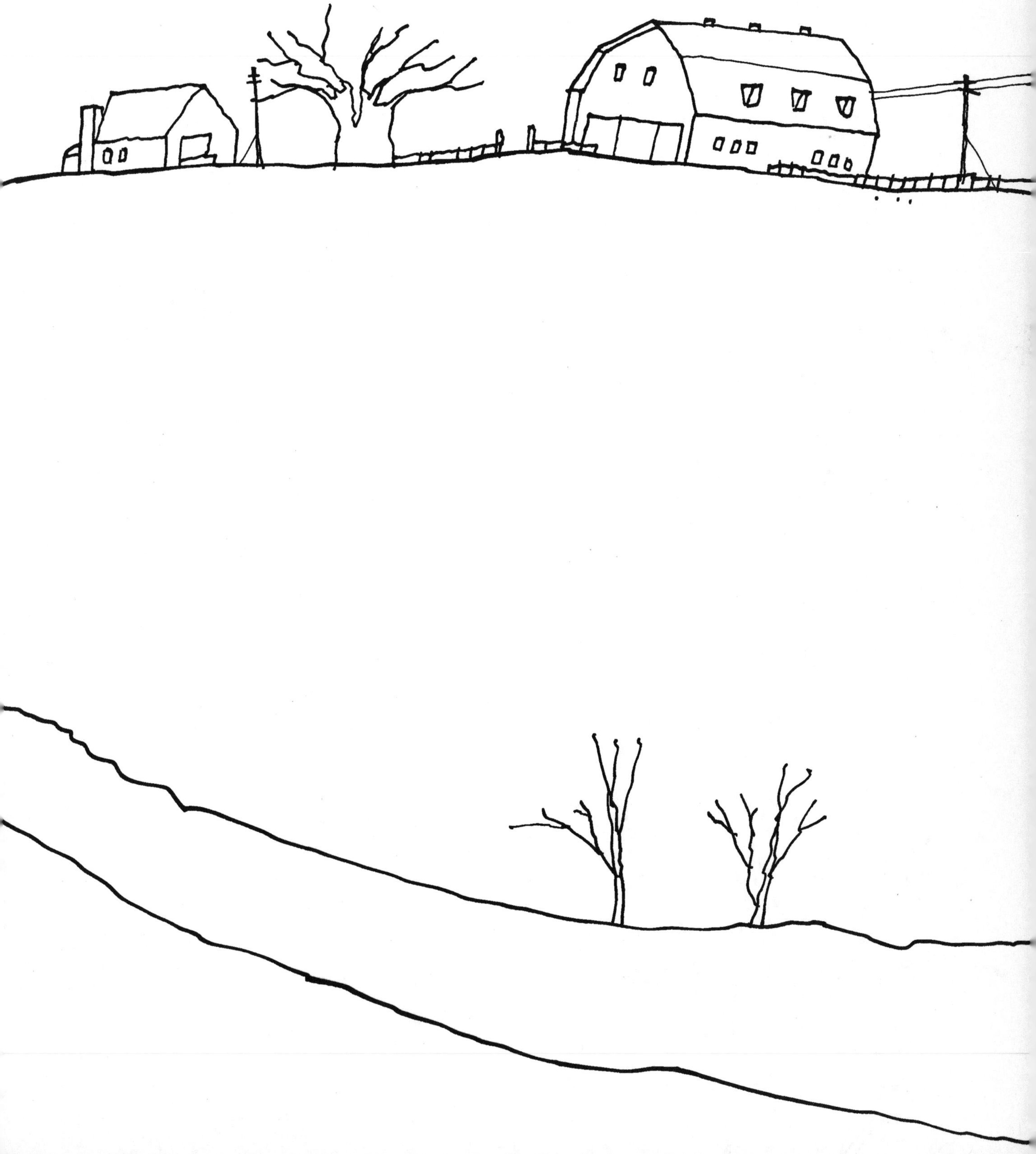

Autumn has come

Now what are people doing?

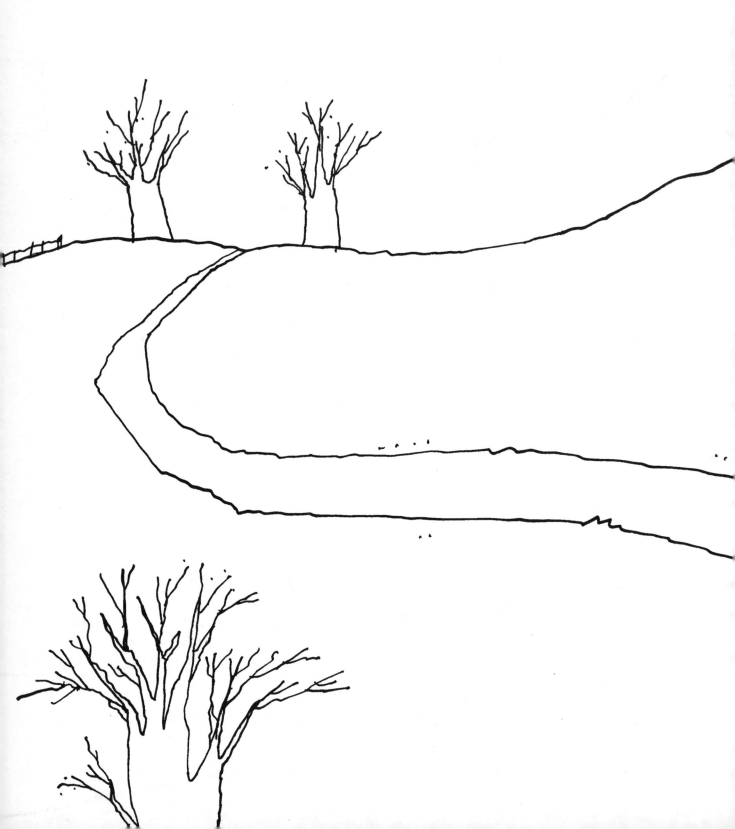

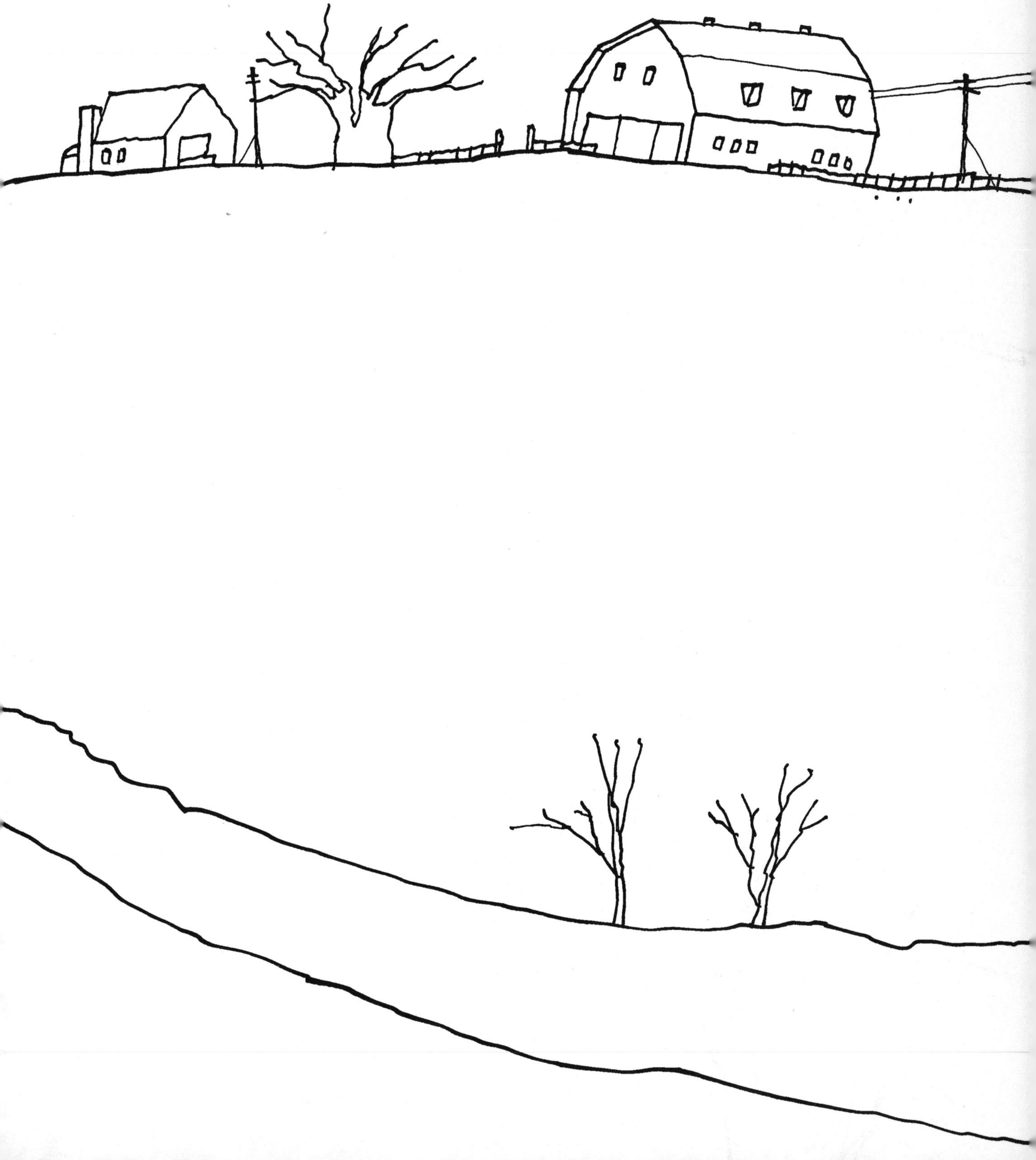

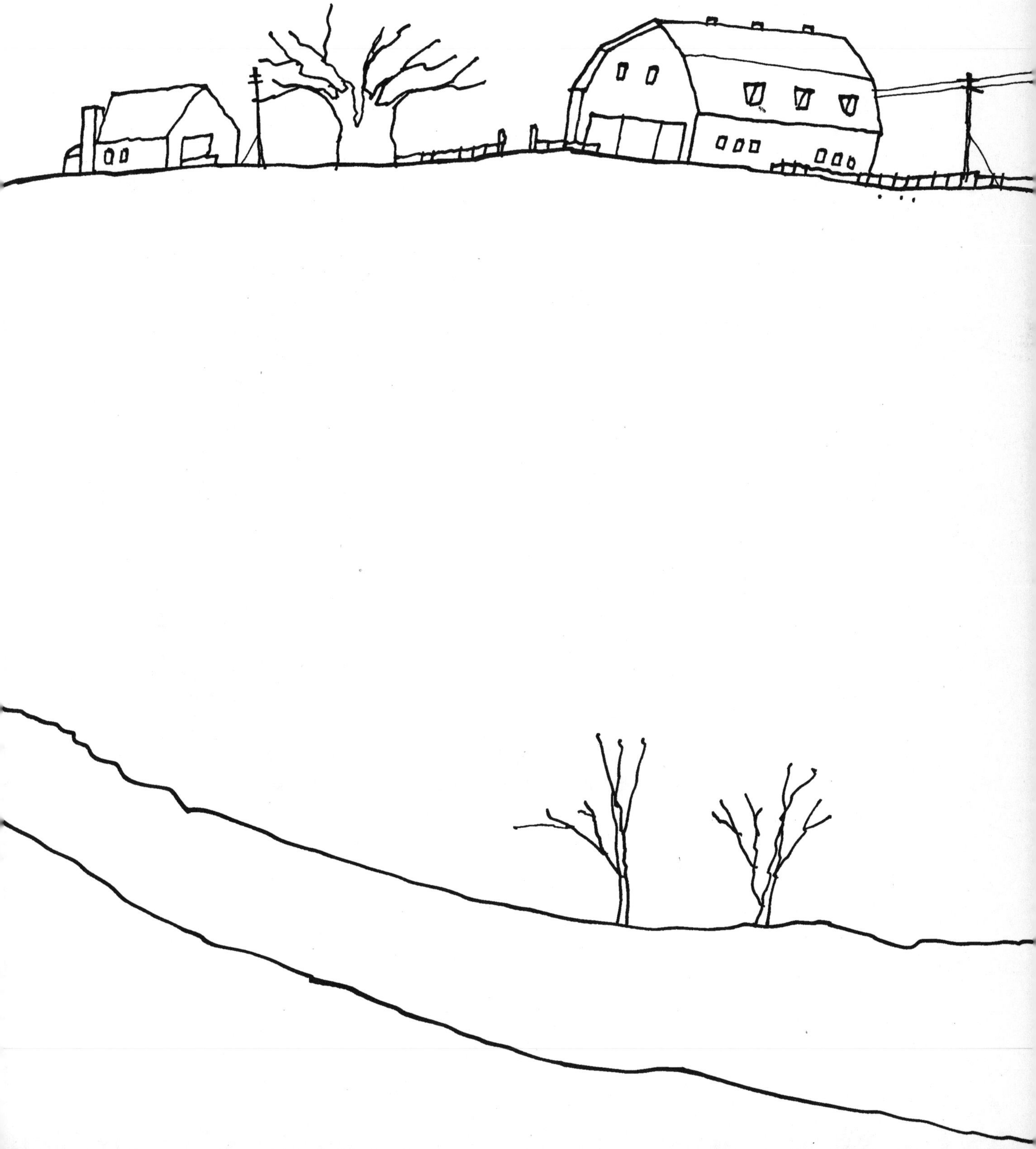

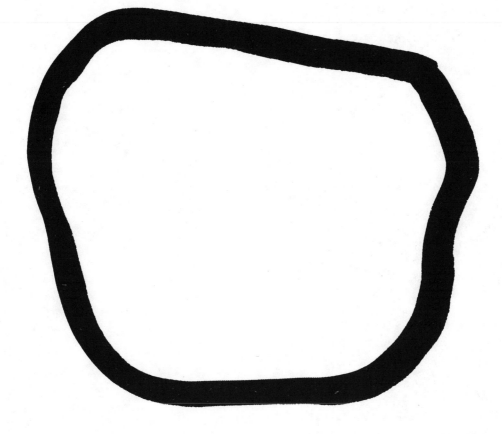

Draw a snowball fight

(After 'cat', draw something beginning with 't')

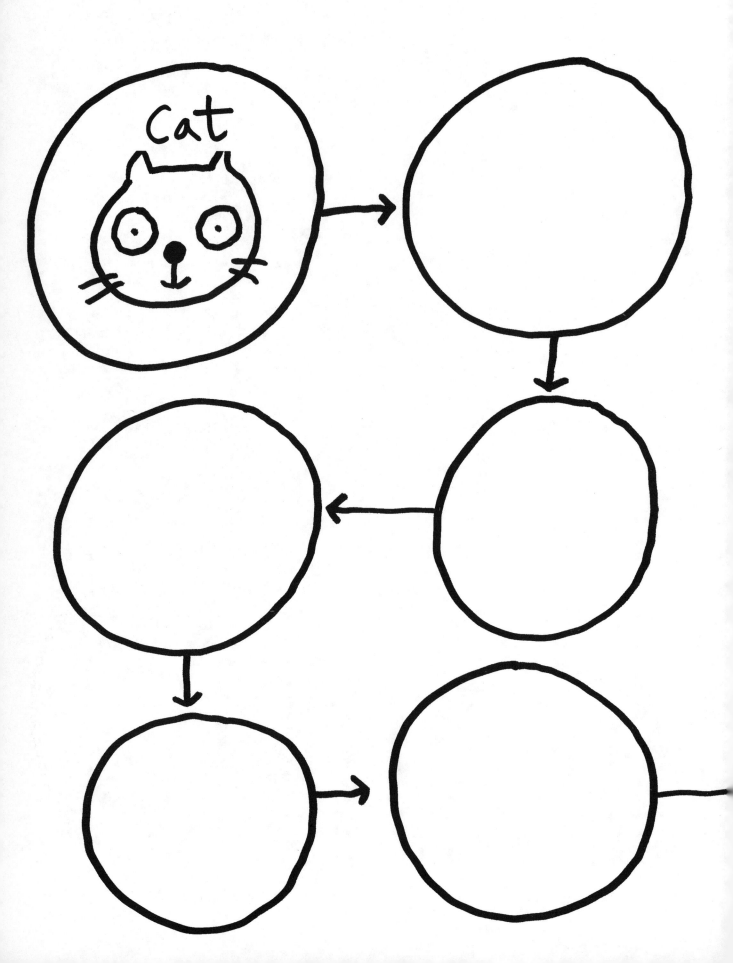

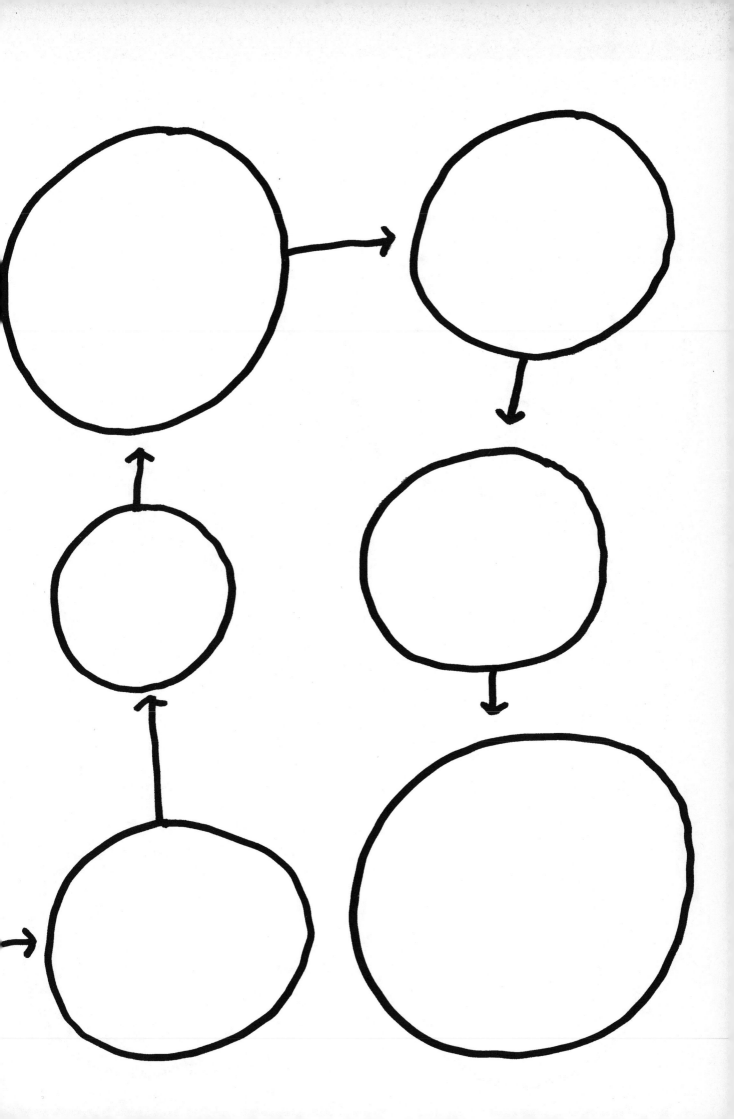

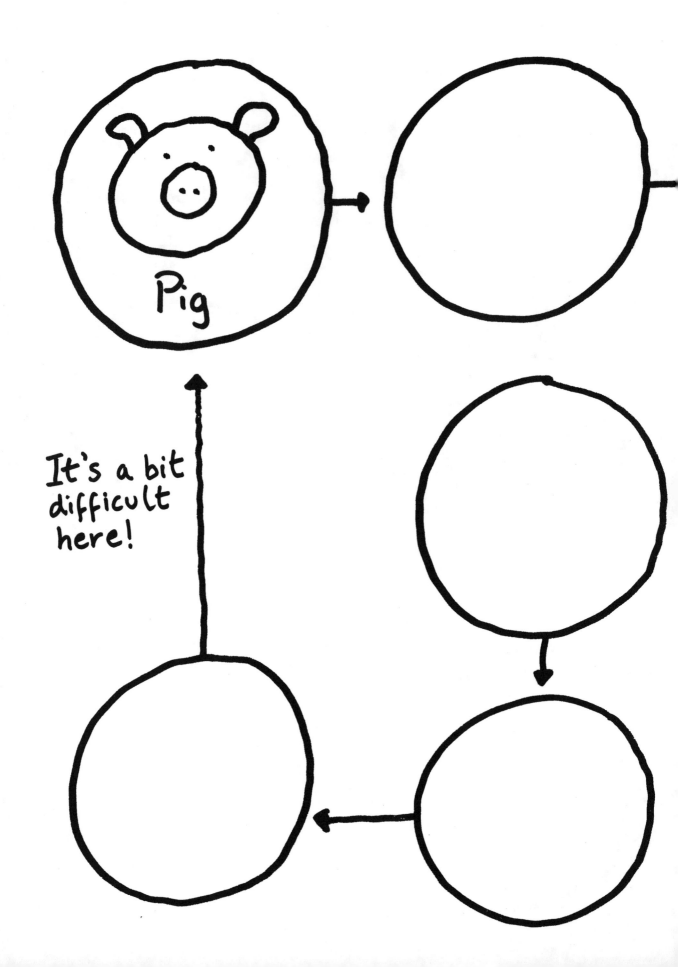

Pig

It's a bit difficult here!

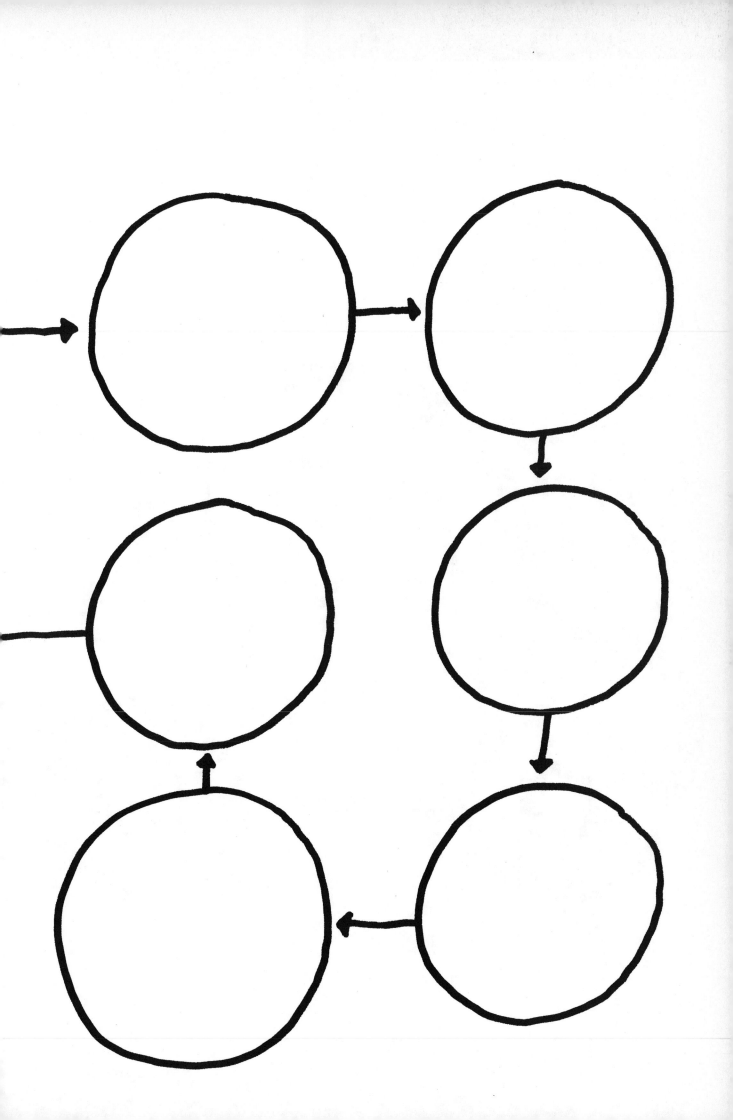

Here are some very old cars

Colour them

Here is a spray-paint fight

Don't try this at home!

John	Michael	Ella
Anna	Thomas	Rebecca
Lou	Sunita	Jude

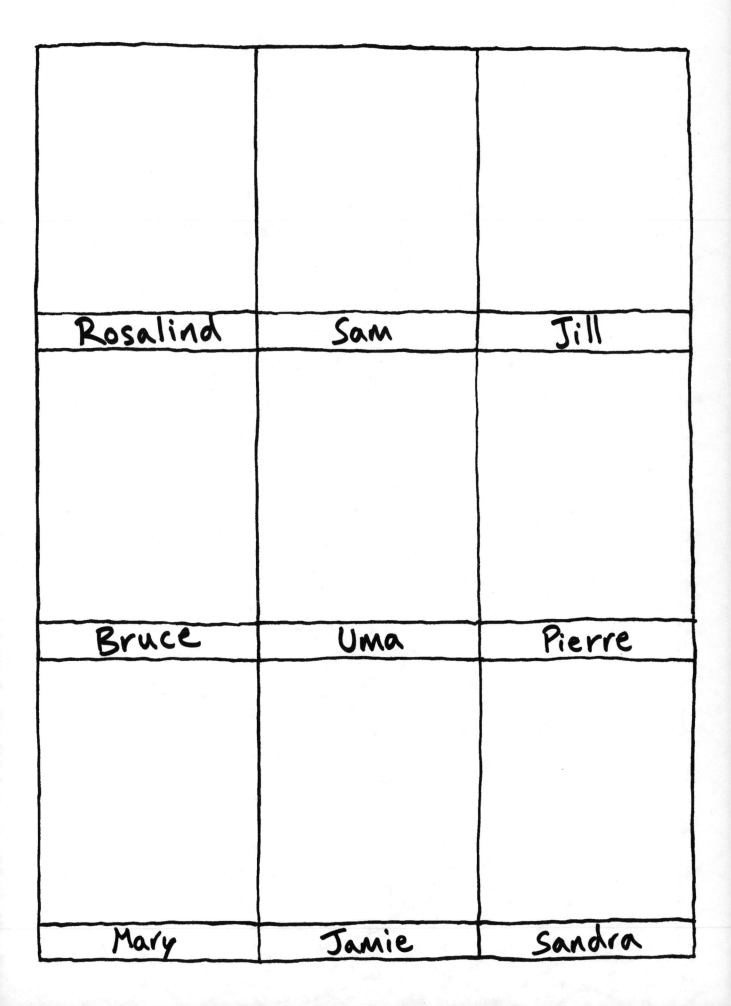

Rosalind	Sam	Jill
Bruce	Uma	Pierre
Mary	Jamie	Sandra

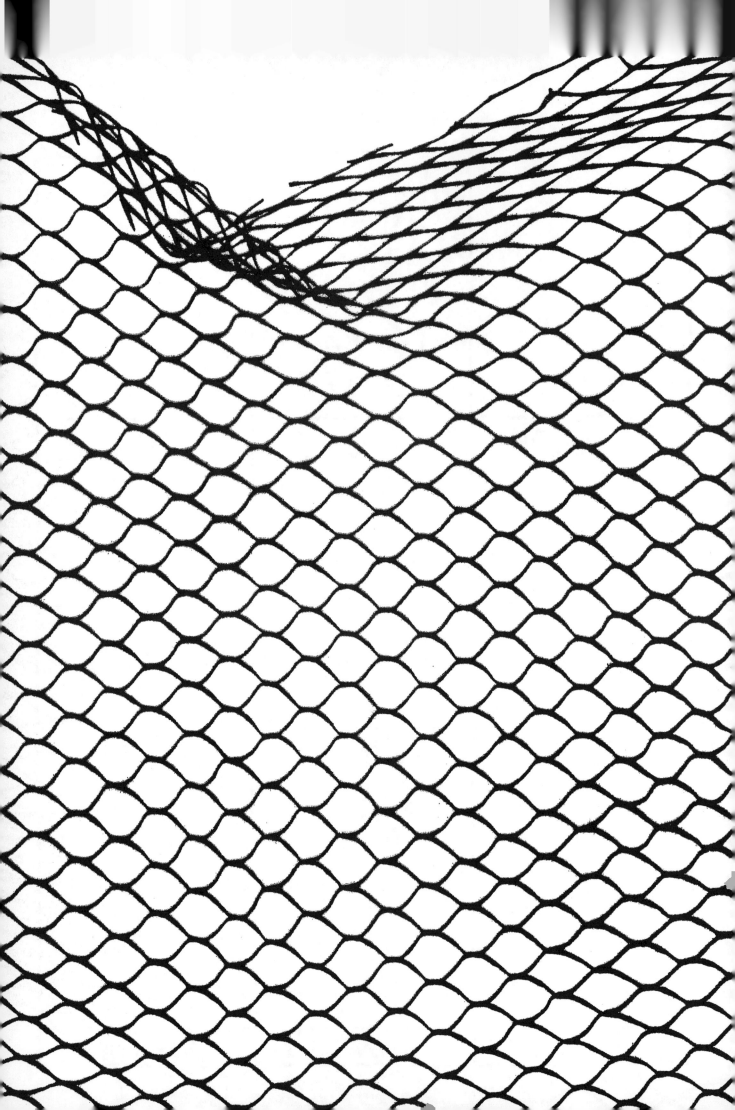

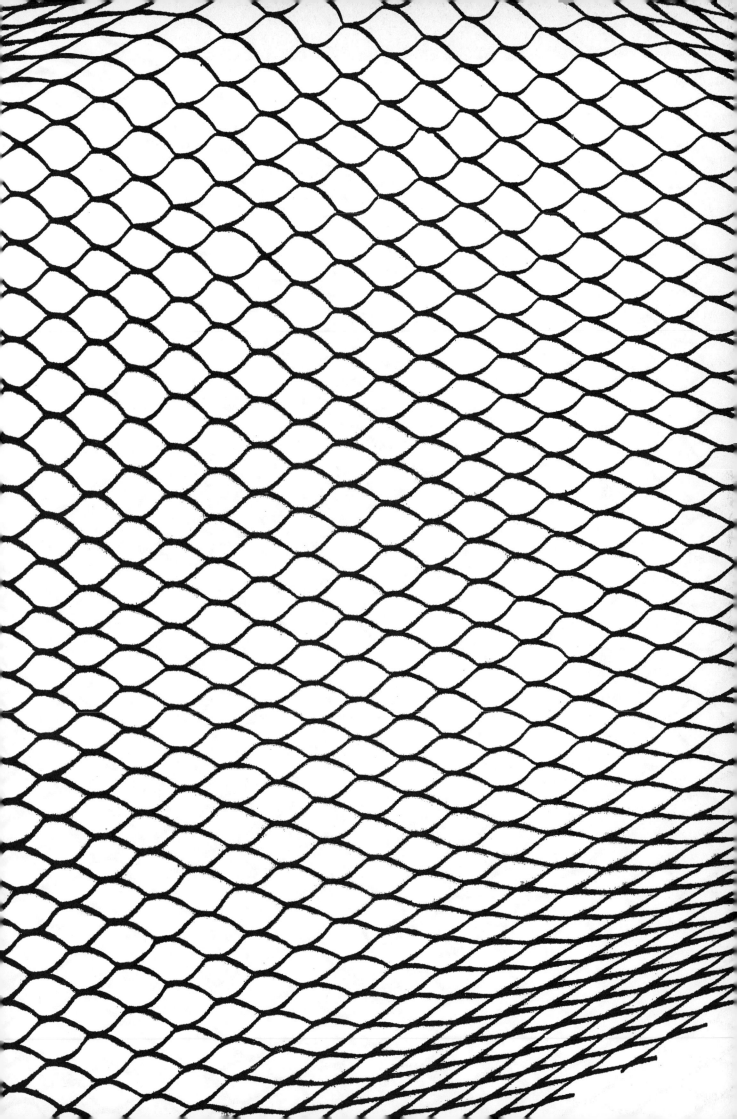

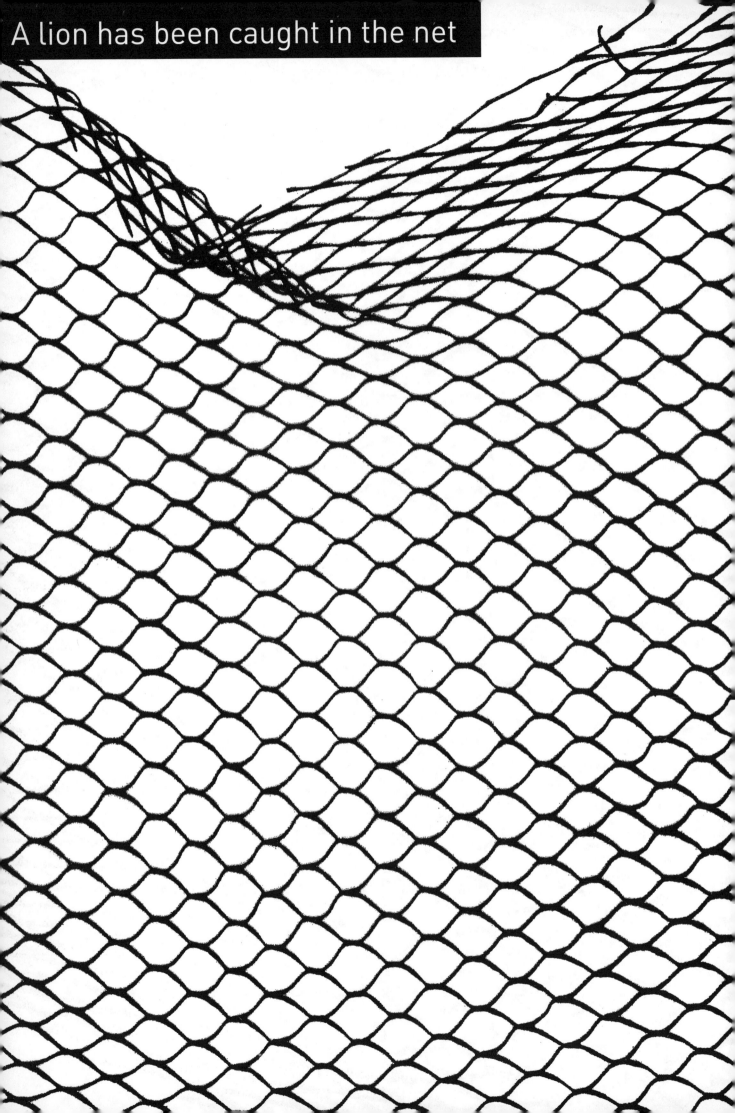

A lion has been caught in the net

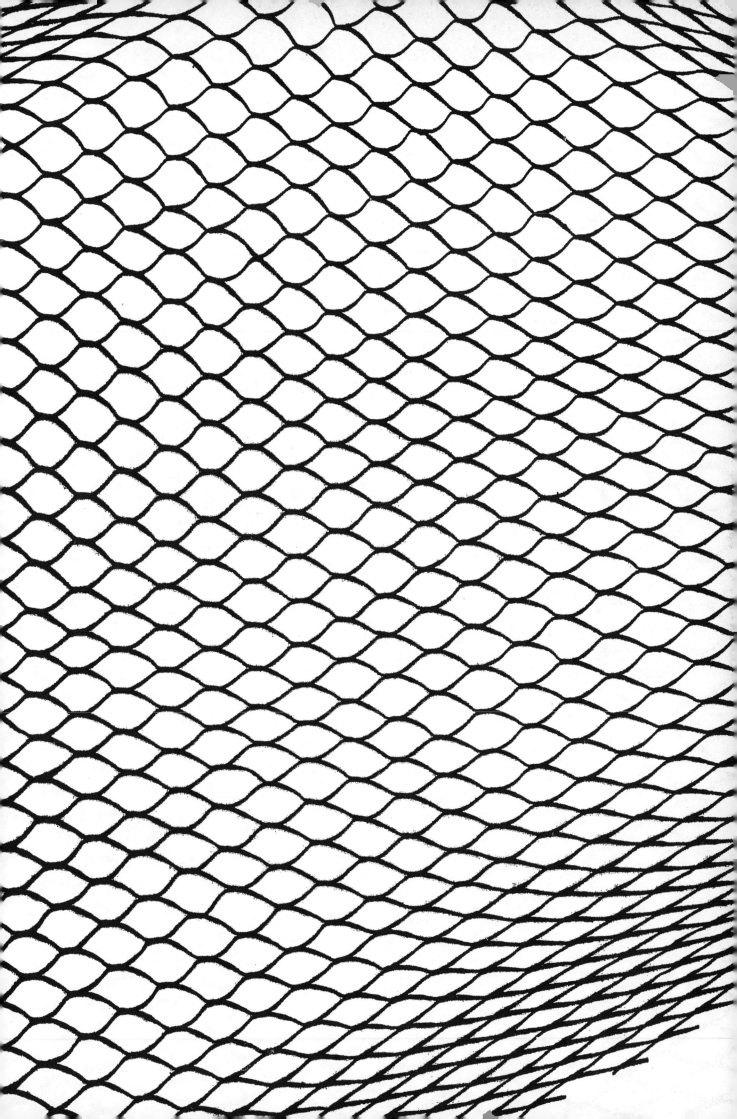

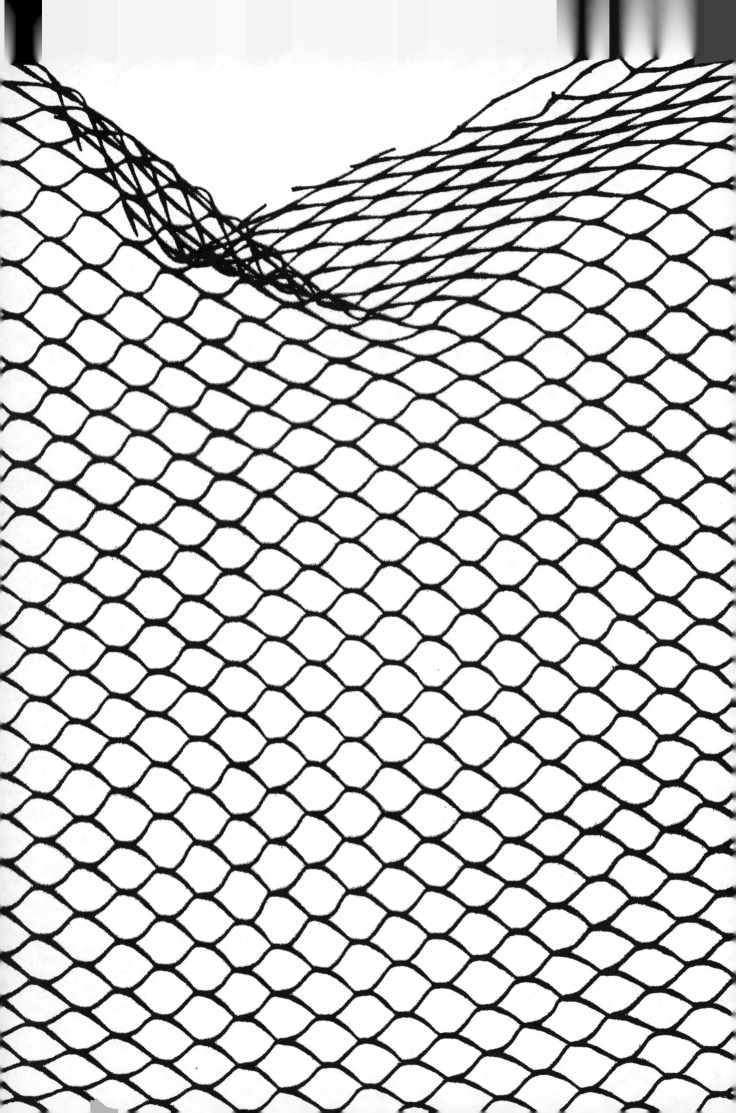

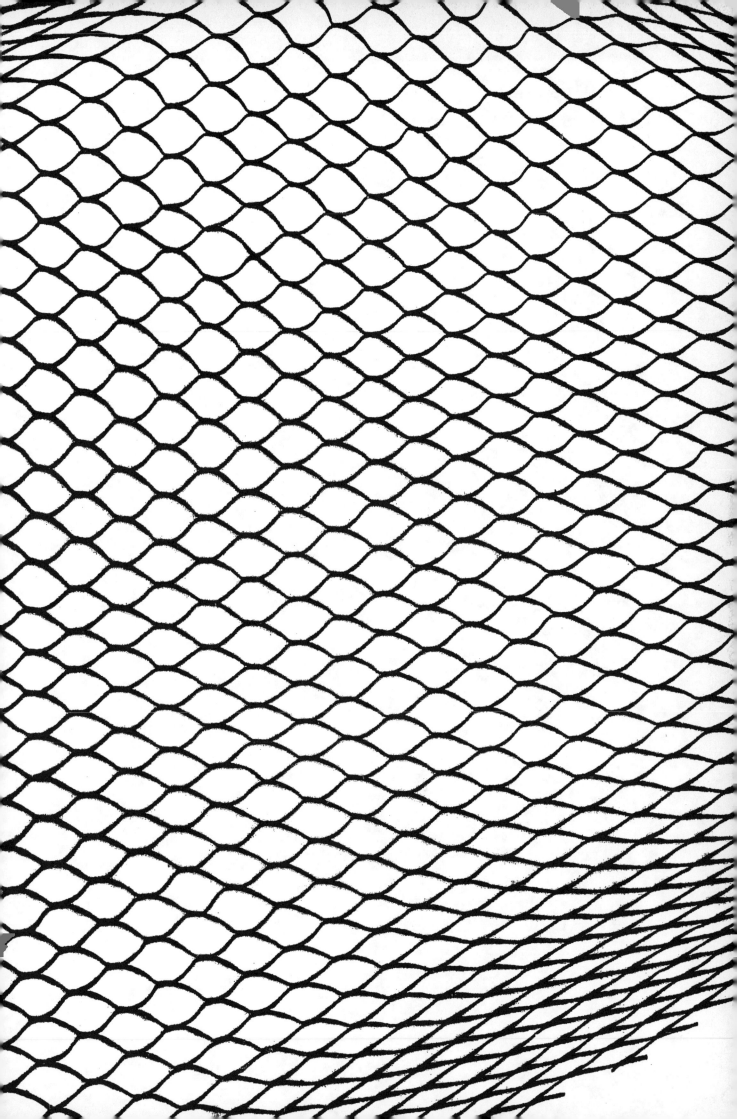

This is a wild horse

Can you calm him down?

Draw the people watching

Make them pretty

Paint the wall with your friend

Use the same colour please!

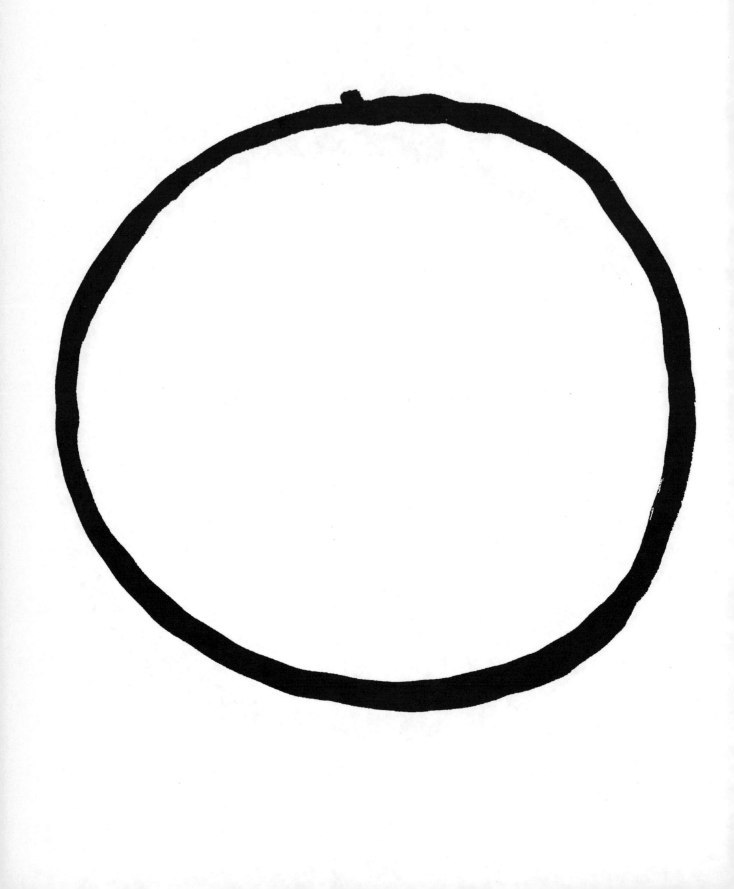

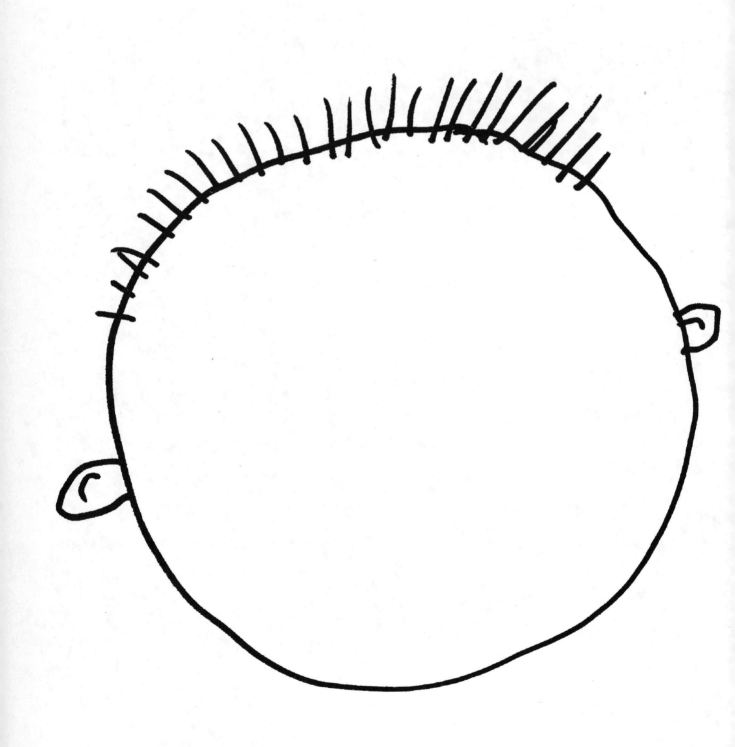

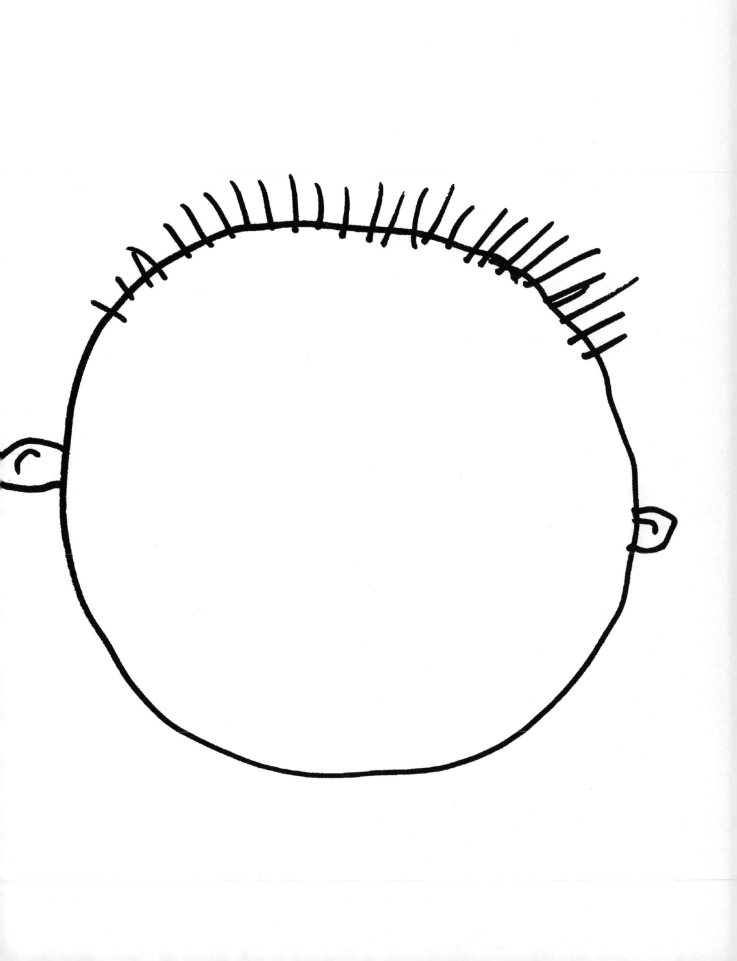

$$46 \overline{) 16790}$$

Mark these answers

Five points for every
right answer

1. $15+18=23$

2. $30-6=14$

3. $20+20+15=85$

4. $30-3=27$

5. $50 \div 2 = 24$

6. $23+8=41$

7. $35 \times 2 + 1 = 71$

8. $8+2+9+2+4=22$

9. $5-2+4+2+8=3$

10. $600 \div 30 = 50$

11. $200 \div 10 + 2 - 1 = 21$

12. $(5+38) \times 2 = 88$

13. $20 \div 3 = 7.1$

14. $9+5 \times 12 \div 3 = 29$

15. $4+5=9$

16. $9-2=7$

17. $6+3=10$

18. $10-2-2 \quad 5$

19. $18 \div 3 = 8$

20. $900+25-23+6-4=$
903

Number of correct answers	Total

C·5 – K·5 – I·9 – H·5 – F·8 – J·7 – I·1 – F·5 – G·5 (Can you guess what it's going to be?) D·4 – K·3 – I·4 – K·7 – I·8 – E·7 – F·4 – F·2 (Any ideas?) I·6 – J·5 – J·8 – D·6 – I·2 – K·4 – F·7 – E·5 (Keep colouring...) F·3 – I·7 – I·3 – D·5 – E·3 – E·6 – F·6 – J·3 (Almost there...) J·6 – J·2 – E·4 – J·4 – I·5 (The last one!) K·6

	1	2	3	4	5	6	7	8	9
A									
B									
C									
D									
E									
F									
G									
H									
I									
J									
K									
L									

E·6 – H·8 – J·7 – B·8 – D·2 – B·4 – F·4 – J·8 – C·6 – G·6 (Can you make out a shape?) J·2 – L·3 – D·8 – F·2 – B·2 – L·8 – G·4 – B·6 – C·4 – C·5 – F·8 – I·6 – I·8 – H·6 – E·2 – C·7 – E·7 – D·6 – H·2 (Have you guessed what it is yet?) C·2 – K·2 – K·8 – L·2 – C·8 – F·6 – C·3 – I·4 – E·5 – D·4 – G·8 – I·7 – J·3 – I·2 – G·3 – E·4 – E·8 – G·7 (Just a few more to go…) I·5 – K·7 – G·2 – G·5 – H·4 – K·3 – E·3 – I·3 – L·7

	1	2	3	4	5	6	7	8	9
A									
B									
C									
D									
E									
F									
G									
H									
I									
J									
K									
L									

It's so hot!

Draw something to cool them down

Can you wrap up the fish in foil?

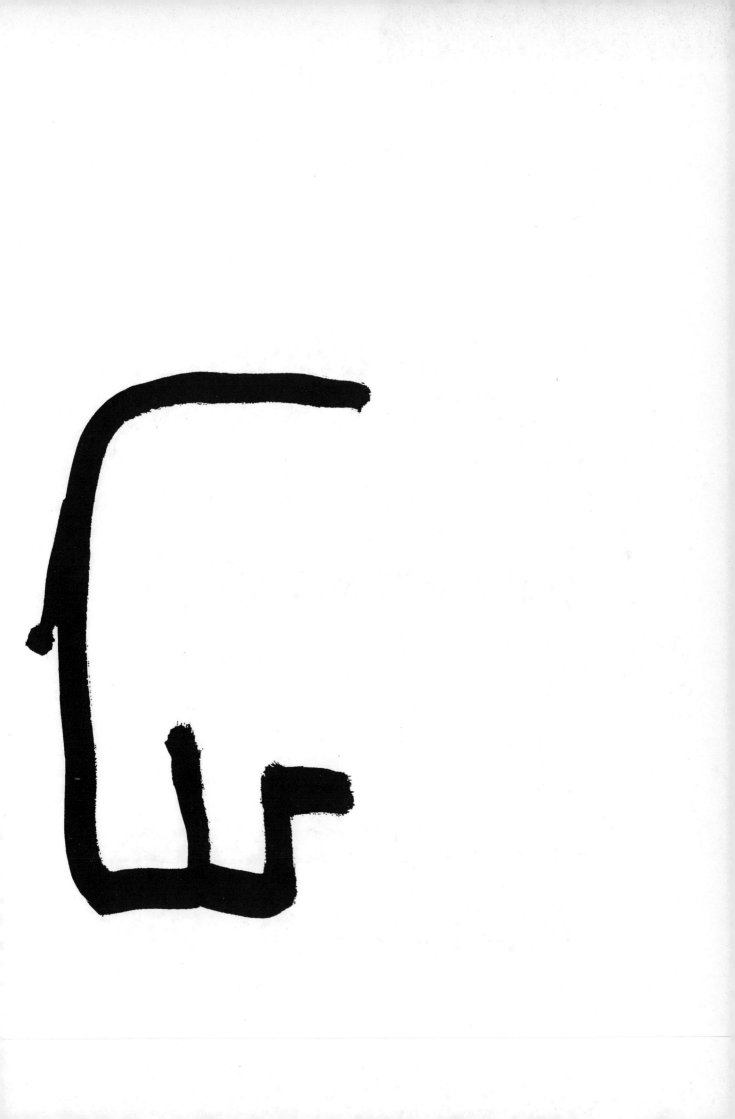

Add plenty of fillings

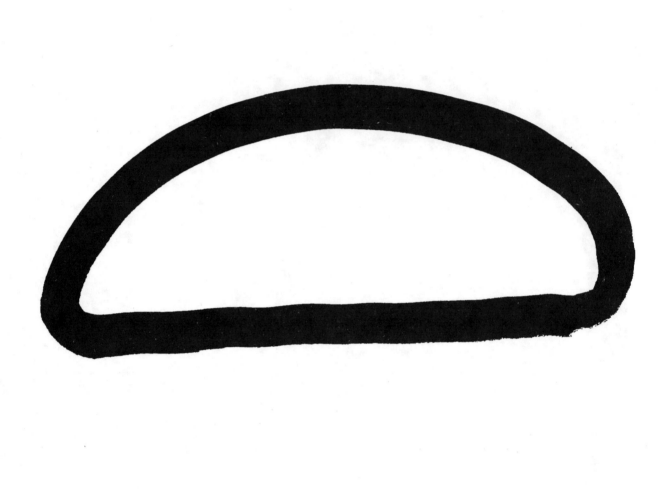

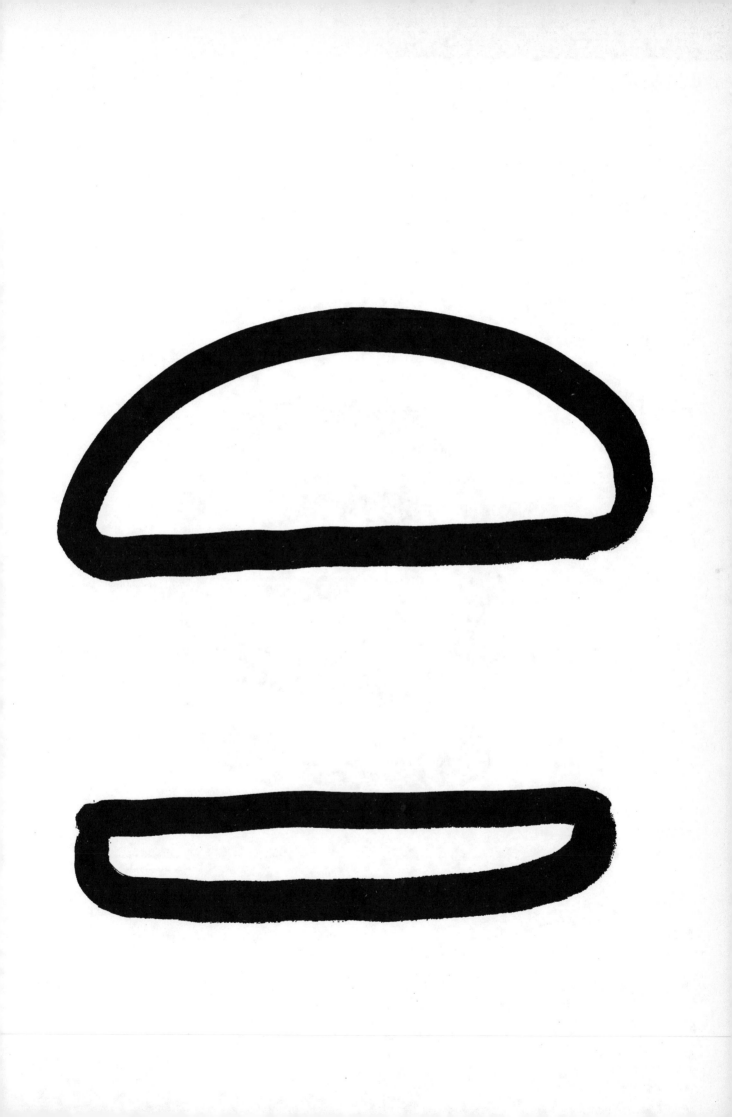

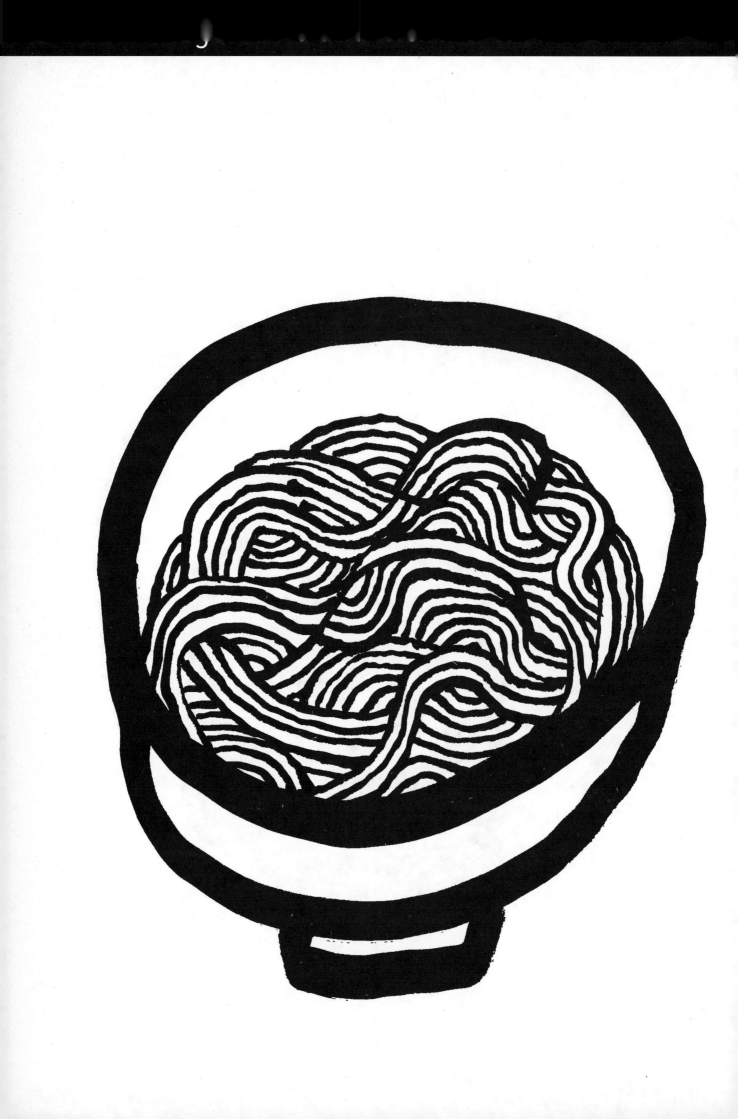

Here are sunbathers on a beach

Give each person a nice tan

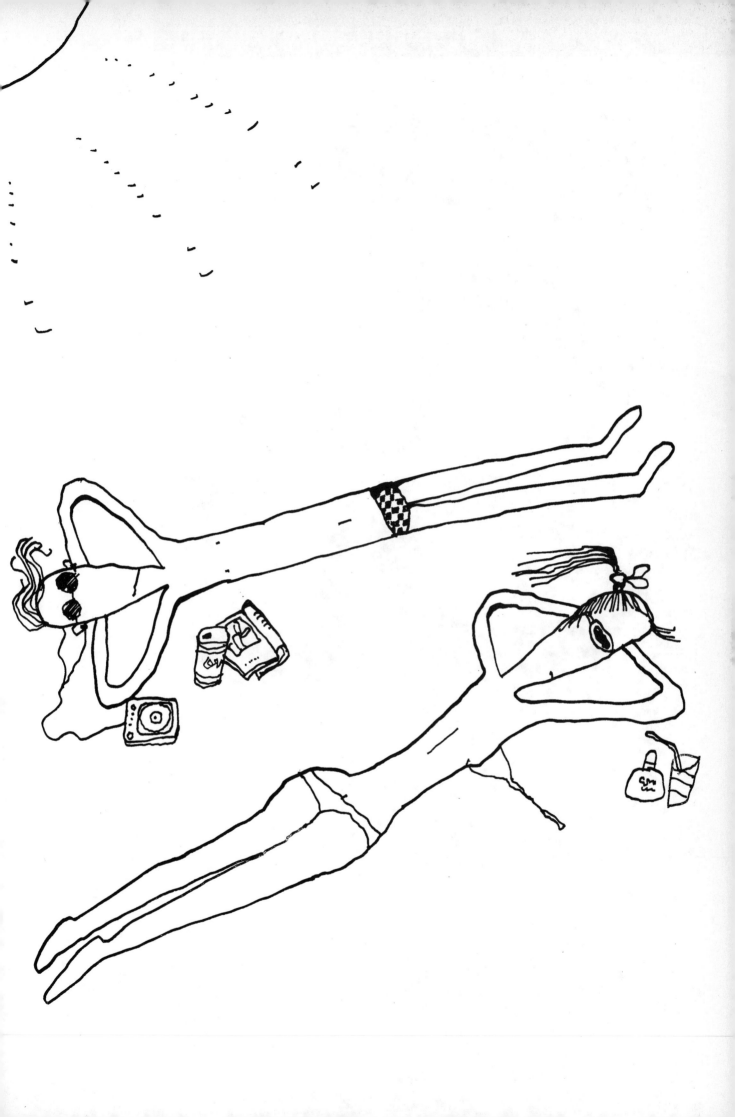

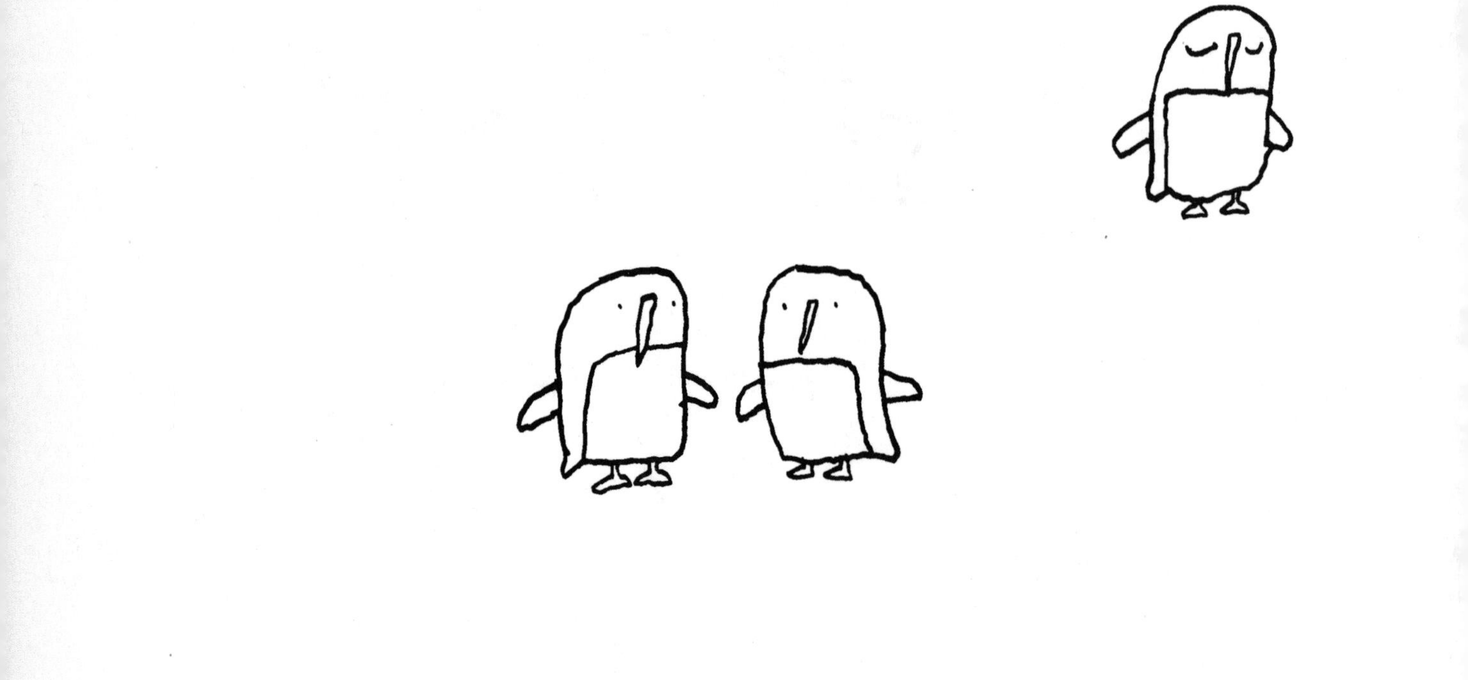

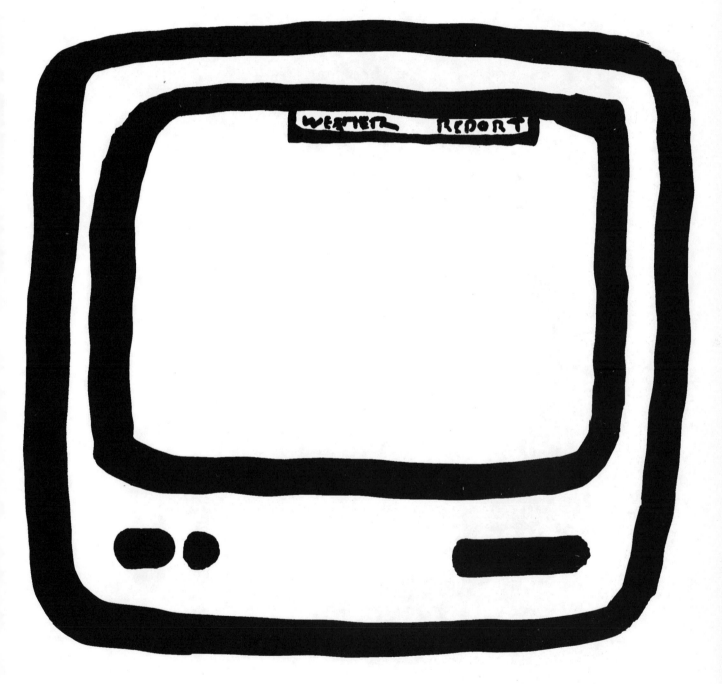

WEATHER REPORT

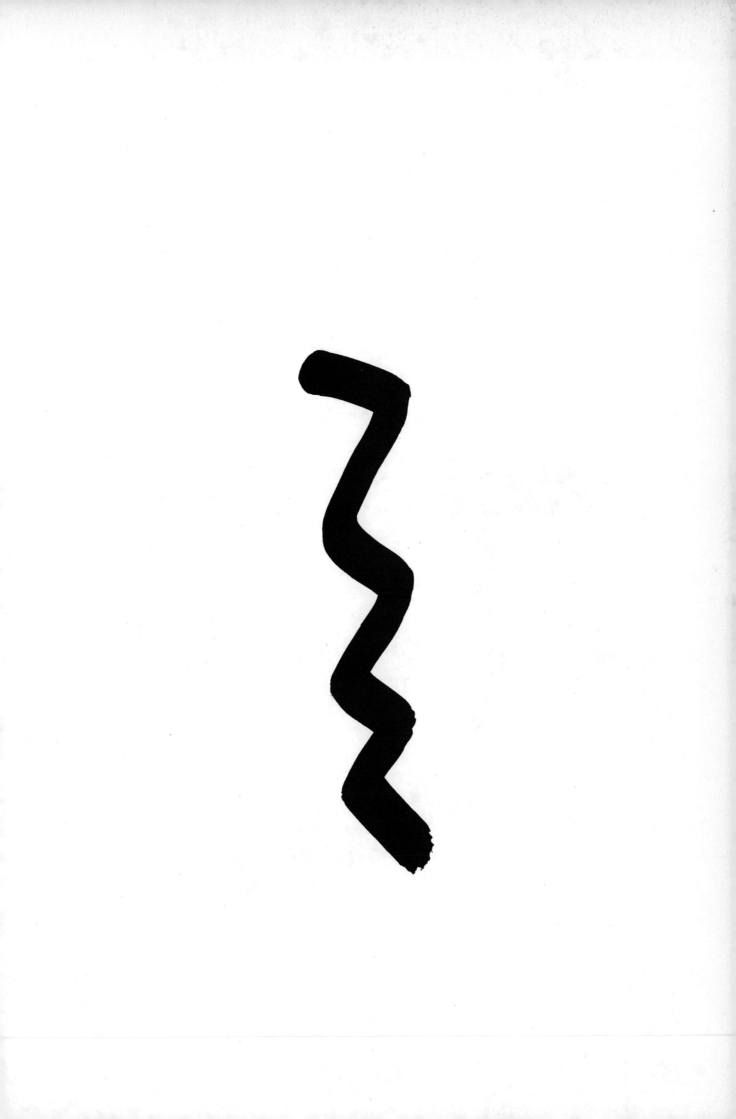

These are stereo speakers

Can you draw some loud music?

These are music boxes

Can you draw the tunes they are playing?

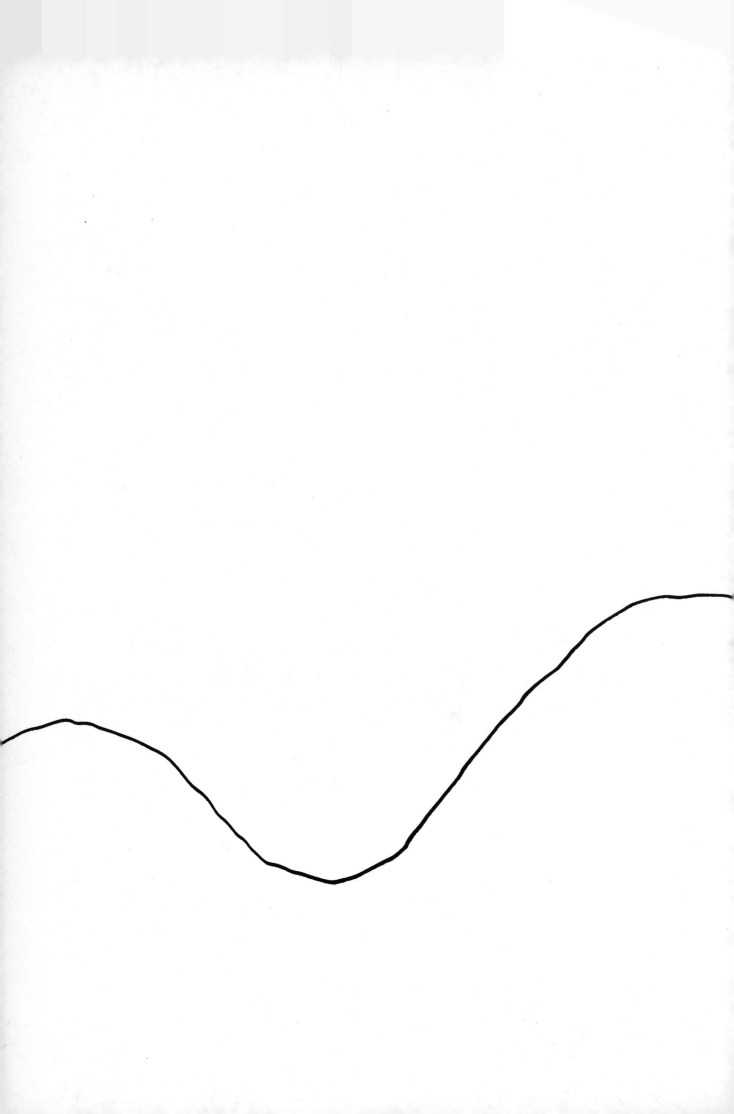

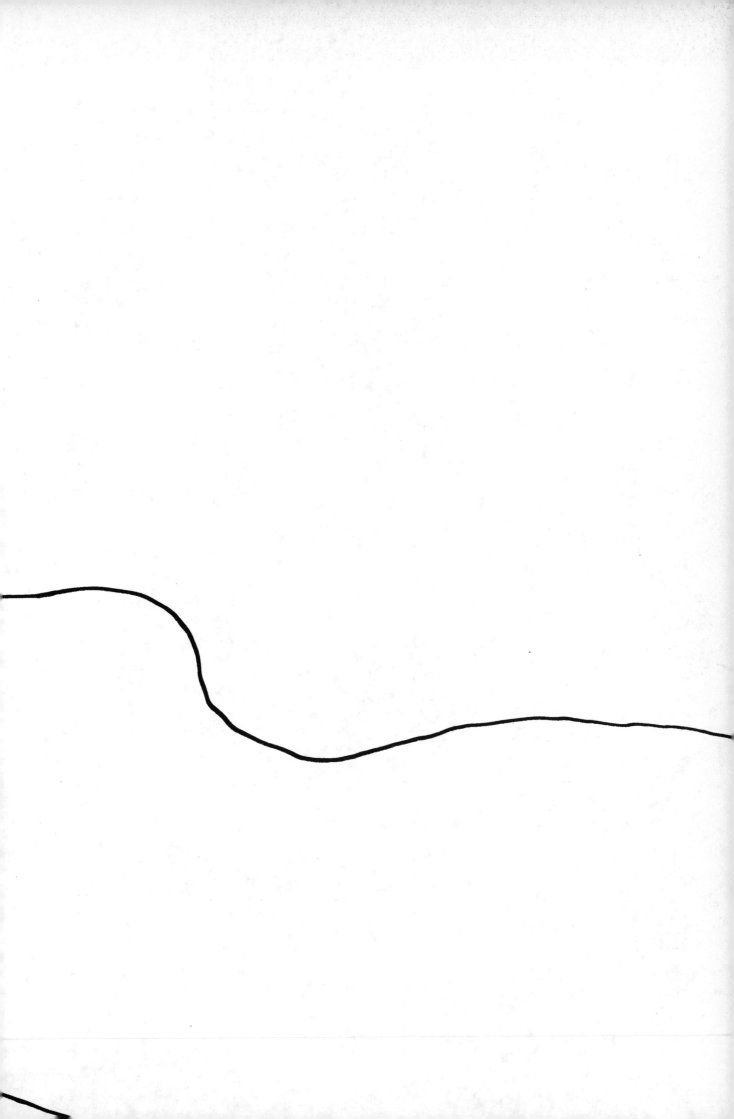

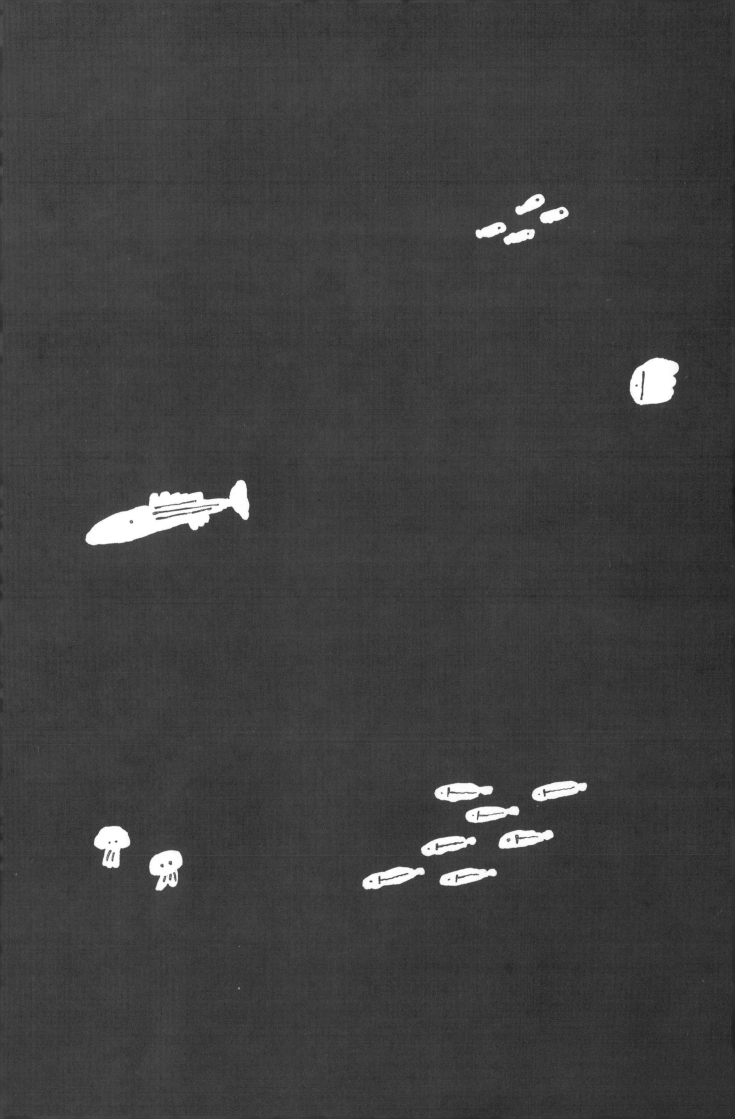

This is an aquarium

Draw something in each tank

Spotty whale

Multicoloured fish

This is a zoo

Draw an animal in each cage

Long-legged
cat

stripy bear

This is a botanical garden

Draw some plants

Snaky
palm
tree

THUD!

GONG !

Ratatatat!

Clickety-click!

OUCH !

Psst!

SPLAT!

Quack quack!

Grr!

Shh! —

Tick-tock, tick-tock

Colour the dinosaurs

Make them look fierce

Find the words

Search from left to right, right to left, up and down, even diagonally!

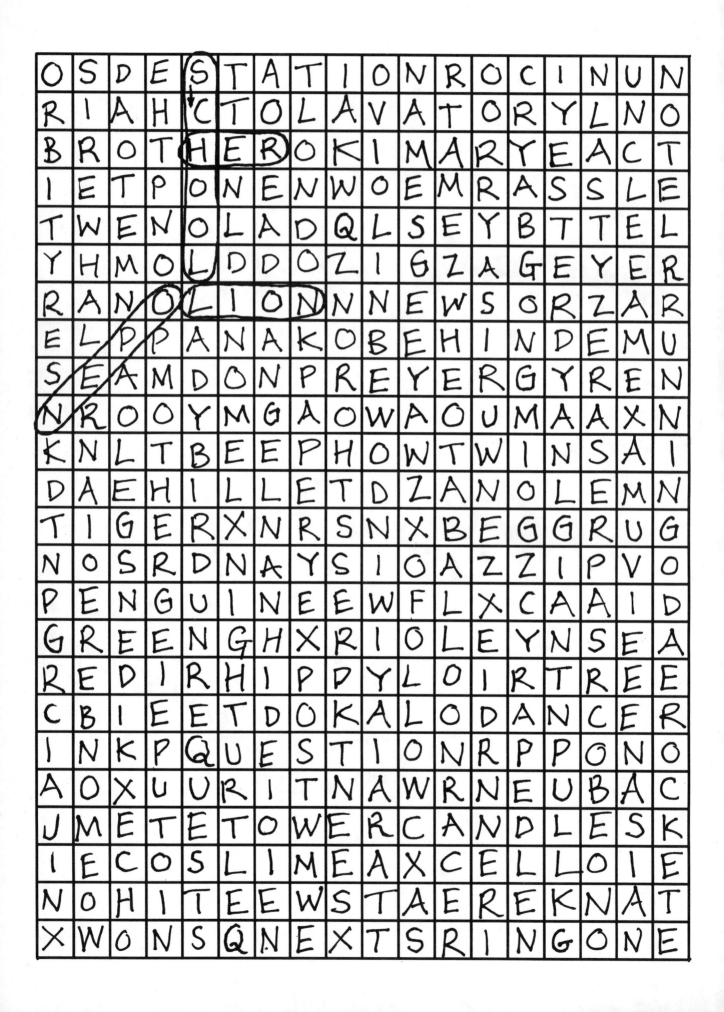

O	S	D	E	S	T	A	T	I	O	N	R	O	C	I	N	U	N
R	I	A	H	C	T	O	L	A	V	A	T	O	R	Y	L	N	O
B	R	O	T	H	E	R	O	K	I	M	A	R	Y	E	A	C	T
I	E	T	P	O	N	E	N	W	O	E	M	R	A	S	S	L	E
T	W	E	N	O	L	A	D	Q	L	S	E	Y	B	T	T	E	L
Y	H	M	O	L	D	D	O	Z	I	G	Z	A	G	E	Y	E	R
R	A	N	O	L	I	O	N	N	N	E	W	S	O	R	Z	A	R
E	L	P	P	A	N	A	K	O	B	E	H	I	N	D	E	M	U
S	E	A	M	D	O	N	P	R	E	Y	E	R	G	Y	R	E	N
N	R	O	O	Y	M	G	A	O	W	A	O	U	M	A	A	X	N
K	N	L	T	B	E	E	P	H	O	W	T	W	I	N	S	A	I
D	A	E	H	I	L	L	E	T	D	Z	A	N	O	L	E	M	N
T	I	G	E	R	X	N	R	S	N	X	B	E	G	G	R	U	G
N	O	S	R	D	N	A	Y	S	I	O	A	Z	Z	I	P	V	O
P	E	N	G	U	I	N	E	E	W	F	L	X	C	A	A	I	D
G	R	E	E	N	G	H	X	R	I	O	L	E	Y	N	S	E	A
R	E	D	I	R	H	I	P	P	Y	L	O	I	R	T	R	E	E
C	B	I	E	E	T	D	O	K	A	L	O	D	A	N	C	E	R
I	N	K	P	Q	U	E	S	T	I	O	N	R	P	P	O	N	O
A	O	X	U	U	R	I	T	N	A	W	R	N	E	U	B	A	C
J	M	E	T	E	T	O	W	E	R	C	A	N	D	L	E	S	K
I	E	C	O	S	L	I	M	E	A	X	C	E	L	L	O	I	E
N	O	H	I	T	E	E	W	S	T	A	E	R	E	K	N	A	T
X	W	O	N	S	Q	N	E	X	T	S	R	I	N	G	O	N	E

S	F	L	O	W	E	R	T	E	N	S	H	O	W	S	L	P	S
U	R	I	V	E	R	I	S	P	O	T	A	T	O	E	E	L	N
P	Y	U	C	H	A	I	R	U	D	A	N	S	K	Y	E	E	A
E	U	A	N	I	T	W	O	Z	N	R	T	E	S	T	E	A	K
R	U	H	C	G	R	O	O	D	O	E	R	A	S	E	R	T	E
M	M	T	U	H	B	O	T	T	L	E	M	O	N	A	T	A	N
A	P	O	W	O	T	N	W	N	K	N	O	B	D	X	R	A	Y
N	E	O	A	R	U	U	O	I	O	W	L	I	E	E	L	E	E
S	R	T	I	A	U	S	N	P	L	I	O	N	P	L	I	N	N
G	P	K	I	N	D	G	I	A	I	Z	G	A	L	E	A	I	R
I	S	O	N	G	I	N	A	M	V	G	O	L	A	P	P	L	E
A	T	O	O	E	K	I	U	I	E	Y	A	O	Y	A	R	D	Y
T	A	B	A	N	K	R	O	S	E	M	O	O	N	A	I	L	B
D	T	E	T	A	D	I	P	S	S	I	N	K	C	A	L	L	R
T	I	R	O	N	E	L	E	P	H	A	N	T	A	Z	U	I	O
N	O	A	A	P	R	O	N	D	O	O	F	P	R	E	A	D	W
I	N	B	R	O	W	N	P	O	S	T	O	O	L	A	L	I	N
A	D	B	O	Y	E	N	O	O	P	S	B	O	X	I	I	G	B
P	E	I	Y	E	L	L	O	W	Y	H	P	L	M	A	N	N	E
E	B	T	O	Y	U	G	L	D	A	O	R	A	A	O	E	R	E
T	E	A	R	E	N	O	C	T	A	R	B	C	S	R	W	E	T
N	E	T	K	S	C	Q	U	E	S	T	I	O	N	O	S	T	L
X	C	N	U	S	H	I	P	A	R	K	R	I	B	B	O	N	E
A	I	C	E	C	R	E	A	M	A	M	A	D	D	O	O	D	L	E	S

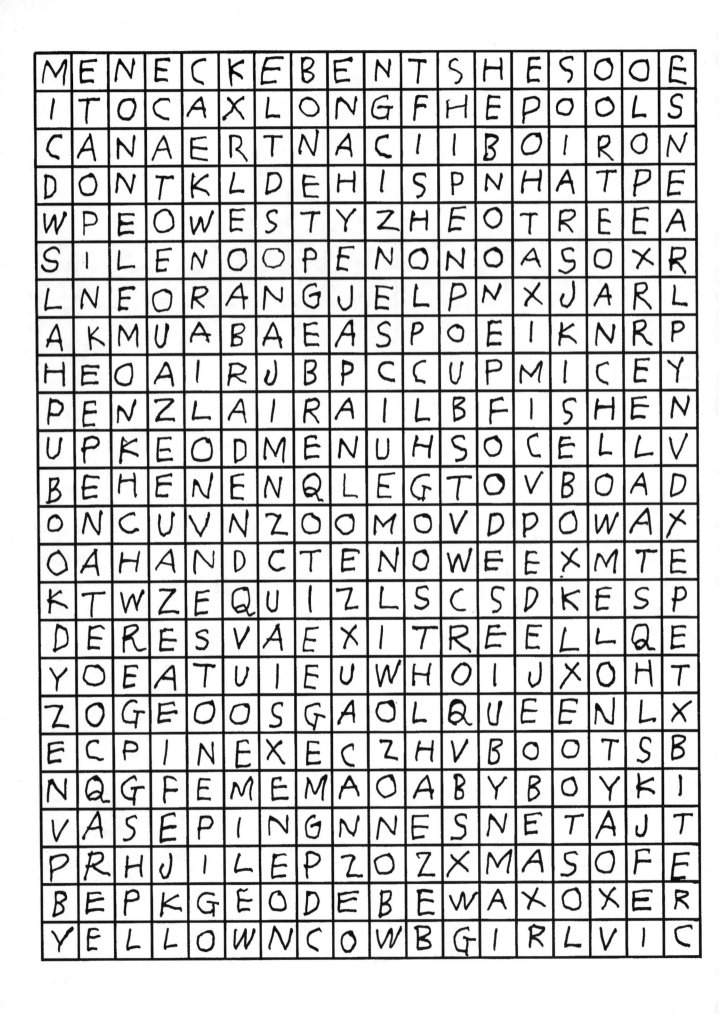

Horizontally, vertically, diagonally – any way you like

2	6	3	9	5	0	2	2	4	3	8	9	0	8	1	4	6	5
3	7	8	5	0	1	2	4	0	8	9	1	2	3	3	4	5	9
9	8	7	3	2	8	6	5	5	4	1	6	5	6	0	1	7	6
1	5	0	1	3	4	7	1	3	6	3	2	4	4	7	6	5	9
6	4	5	3	6	8	2	6	6	0	5	3	5	0	5	3	0	1
0	1	1	6	3	5	2	1	2	6	4	6	4	5	4	2	4	7
6	2	5	9	1	2	6	1	1	1	4	3	2	7	8	1	2	9
3	6	4	6	8	2	6	3	2	4	5	6	7	0	2	3	4	4
1	3	5	0	2	4	8	6	9	2	3	0	3	6	6	5	2	6
8	1	1	2	0	3	4	7	6	4	5	1	2	2	4	3	0	2
9	1	2	9	2	3	0	3	6	4	8	1	2	9	2	4	3	1
1	0	3	5	2	3	1	3	4	3	2	3	6	7	7	3	2	0
2	5	1	2	4	1	8	2	2	8	5	0	5	9	1	6	1	1
1	6	8	2	5	8	4	6	1	5	7	3	7	8	2	3	5	1
4	2	6	2	1	2	3	0	2	7	1	2	6	5	2	8	3	2
6	8	2	4	1	3	1	2	1	1	1	2	4	4	5	2	6	7
3	2	1	5	5	7	3	4	1	9	8	1	0	8	6	7	1	2
7	6	3	6	8	2	2	8	6	3	1	0	2	9	3	4	0	0
1	3	9	2	4	1	0	6	5	3	7	5	4	1	8	1	1	4
1	2	3	6	5	2	1	2	2	5	2	8	3	4	0	2	2	3
2	5	0	2	9	8	4	5	3	10	2	1	5	6	2	7	5	9
9	0	0	0	3	6	0	1	9	1	1	0	6	4	1	5	8	4
1	3	2	1	0	5	2	1	4	2	8	2	5	2	6	7	1	2
0	4	4	2	5	7	3	0	5	6	1	7	2	3	6	2	2	0

Link the stars to form constellations

Check their weight

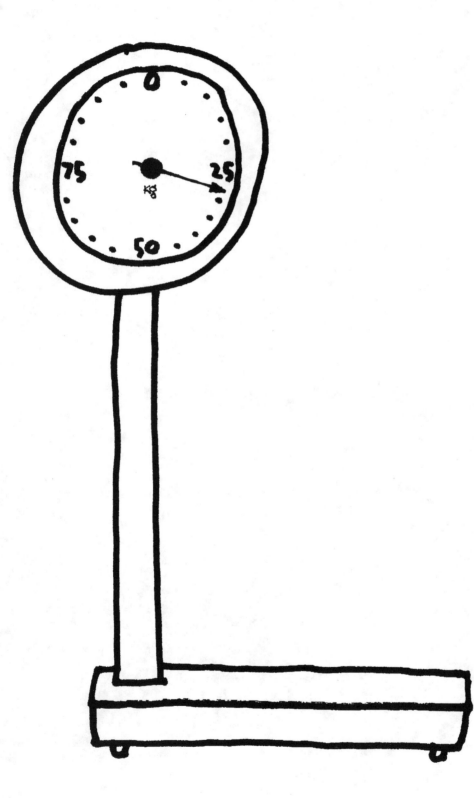

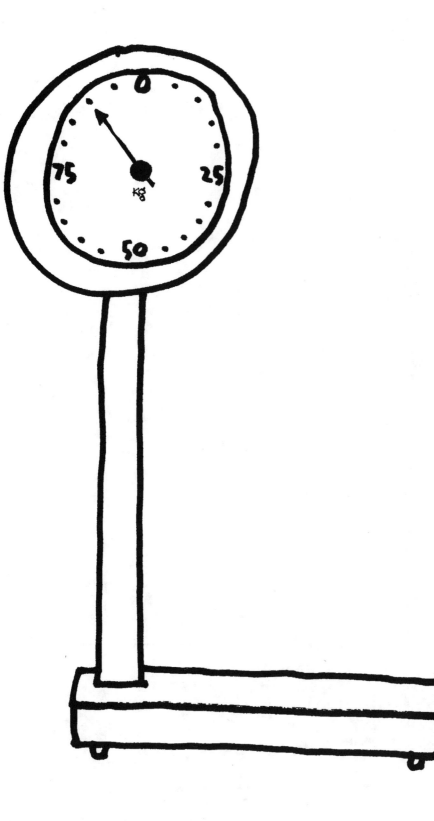

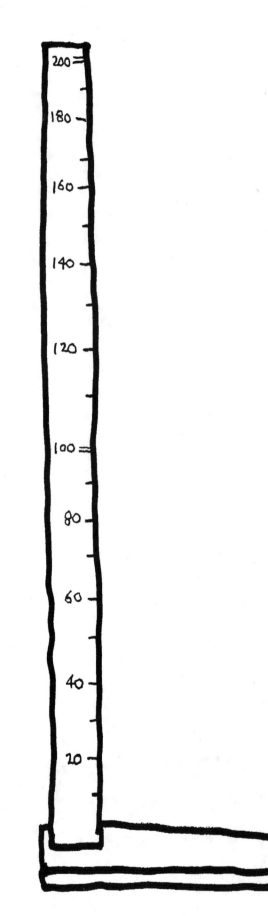

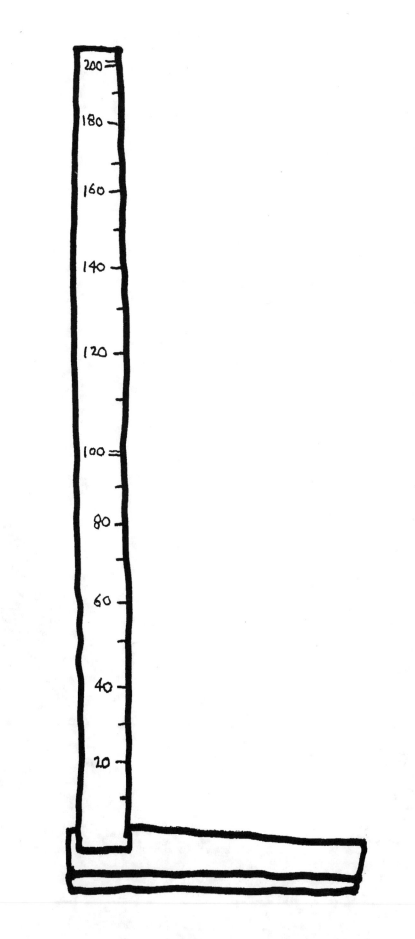

Some unlucky people have fallen into the hole

Draw them

Design the cover and draw the pictures for the story

The Super Duper Scooter

Text by Taro Gomi
Illustrations by ....

SURPRISING! AMAZING! FANTASTIC! MYSTERIOUS!

What is the mysterious
Super Duper Scooter?

Published by
The Doodle Book

This long-awaited picture book is
yours to own at last

· Recommended by
the Association of
Environmentally
Friendly Paper

Written
by a young
genius!

'Where are you going and why are you dressed like that?' asked the badger.
'I'm going to the beach,' replied the fox.

'What are you going to do at the beach?'
'I am going to play with this.'
'What is that?'
'A Super Duper Scooter.'

'What is a Super Duper Scooter? And how do you play with one?'
'I'll show you. Come with me.'
They went to the beach together.

On the beach, the fox started to play with the Super Duper Scooter.
'WOW! It's cool!' The badger was very impressed.

'Let me play, please!' begged the badger.
'Sure. Have a go!'
So the badger tried to play with the Super Duper Scooter.
But...

'Oh noooooooo!'
The badger couldn't do it.
'You are no good.'
The fox could not believe it.
'Oh...' said the badger, disappointed.

The fox felt sorry for the badger and decided to help him.
'Let's do it together,' said the fox.
'Really? Thank you!'
The badger felt very happy.

So the fox and the badger played with the Super Duper Scooter together.

'Oh great! What a fantastic Super Duper Scooter!' screamed the badger.

'I told you it's super,' said the proud fox.

They played with the Super Duper Scooter again and again. It started to get dark and was time to go back home.

The Doodle Book

The best-selling
series includes

① The Marvellous Moped
② The Magical Motorbike
③ The Beautiful Bicycle
④ The Super Duper Scooter (New!)

This is a piece of biscuit

Can you guess what shape it was originally?

This is a piece of bread

Can you guess what shape it was originally?

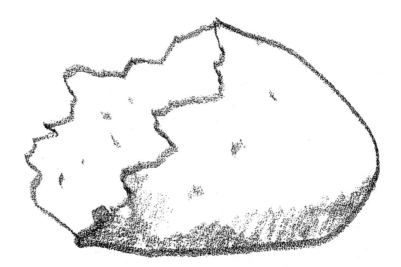

Draw a person using the pencil

Here is a needle and some thread

Draw a person using them

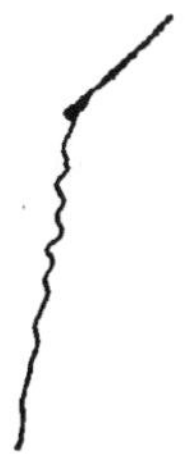

Draw something red

Draw something blue

Draw a scary cushion

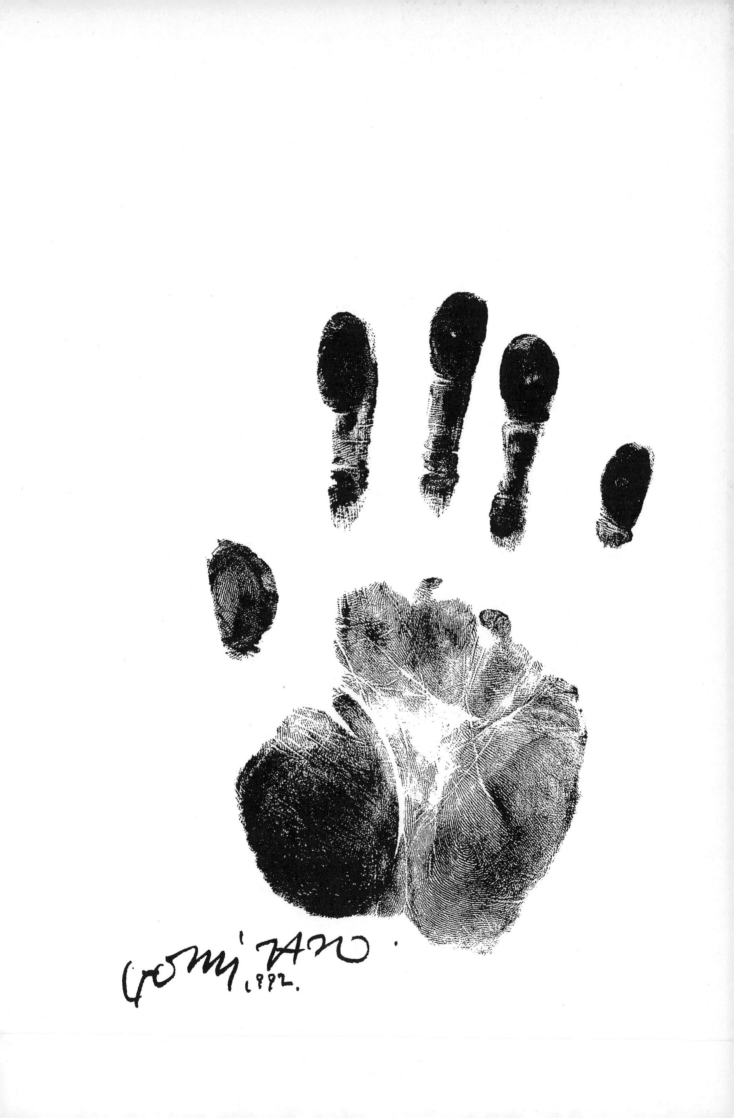